BECOMING A *Titus 2* Mother

ELLA ROSE

TRUTH
BE TOLD

This book is dedicated with love to my wonderful husband Sebastian without whom this book would not be as it is, and to my beautiful children, Theodore, Ava, Ethan, Joy, Patience, and Grace for you have all forever changed me and made me the mother I am and strive to be.

Table of Contents

Acknowledgments

With special thanks:

- To my editor Celeste Ava, for making the necessary tweaks to make this book an easier read, your work is much appreciated.
- To my mother-in-law, Jacqueline Auty, for doing the final last minute read through. You have been a great source of encouragement in my creative endeavours.
- To my first Christian mom friend, Donna Testa, for willingly reading parts of this book before it was complete. Your friendship has been a blessing.
- To my sister Gemma Vernon, for praying for our family. You have shown me strength and courage, even in the toughest of times.
- To my sister Toni Vernon, for reading the very rough draft and very first iteration, and helping make the first few chapters punctually correct. You have been such a warm, loving sister I am glad to also call you friend.
- To my Mother, Sharon Vernon, for teaching me of sacrifice and to dream. You have always aimed to support even my wackiest ideas.
- To my children, Joy and Patience, for teaching me the true blessing of life. Your short lives made a profound impact on our family and we look forward to meeting you one day in heaven.
- To my children on Earth Theodore, Ava, Ethan, and Grace, for loving your father and me even when our imperfections cause strife, I pray that your parenting journey is made easier through our oppeness.
- To my husband Sebastian Roussel, for editing this with me, facing the rough drafts and countless iterations, the late nights and early mornings studying scripture with me. You have helped me stay true, learn and grow. I feel so blessed to be partners with you in this life.

Preface

I never could have imagined being a Christian and happily married with four living children, nor would I have imagined sitting here writing this book. I grew up in a world where my philosophy of life came from friends, family, and TV. I watched shows such as True Blood, Vampire Diaries, and Charmed, so coming to Christ was not on my radar. I had no idea who he was and is. I once performed in a nativity play at school, but I just thought it was some story that schools perform. This is most likely due to the un-biblical additions made by the school to accommodate the numerous students involved in the production. It also didn't help that my eldest sister was sucked into a few cult-like churches, telling her younger sister she was going to hell if she didn't repent. I was five, I was pretty darn scared. After this, my parents told her to never bring such nonsense into our house again. So, she did what all good Christians do: she prayed. She prayed for all of us to know God and come to Christ. It took a good twenty-plus years, but her prayer was answered when my husband and I came to faith, followed by my younger sister and mother.

My Why

When I began writing this book, I hadn't planned to publish it. I was writing because I wanted to explore, investigate, and learn everything I could about being a godly woman. I wanted to get to know God, read His word, and gain a better understanding of Christ. I searched for how to be a Christian woman, and I kept hearing about the Titus 2 Woman. At first, I was confused. I didn't know, nor had I read the book of Titus. So, when I realized it was in the Word, I opened up my Bible and began to read. I was convinced that this was the woman I needed to find. I searched in my life, but everyone around me was either a babe in Christ or still had young children at home. I began to long for this much older woman in the faith with the attributes described by Paul. I started to write and study about the Titus 2 woman described by Paul. I became convicted, determined to try and take on these characteristics and learn to be this woman, for myself and for my daughter. This book developed into a call for us to start taking on the Titus 2 Woman traits now, because frankly, many of us don't have these women around for us to look to. We are the model for our daughters, and I felt that she needed me to go on this quest too. This journey has transformed me and my mothering; it has changed my marriage and my outlook on life so much that I felt I ought to share what I have learned. I pray the pages to come serve you well.

SISTER IN CHRIST

As your fellow Mama, I want to stress here that the contents of this book are not meant as a strict rulebook but rather as a book of ideas and mentorship, a guide if you will, to view motherhood and the world differently and biblically. I am no scholar or theologian; I am a mother who found a deep need for something that was lacking. That being said, I urge you to use your discernment and not make an idol out of me, this book, or any other book for that matter. We are all wonderfully made with our own set of unique ideas, outlooks, and perspectives based on our own experiences. We should look to one another as sisters in Christ.

READING THE BIBLE IN CONTEXT

Before we begin on this journey, I must urge you to be diligent when reading your bible. When you read any verse or chapter of any book, you should try to discern:

- How it fits within that book?
- Where it is in the bible?
- Who wrote it?
- To whom are they speaking? Or who was it written for?
- Why was it written?
- What is the purpose of the writing?

My husband and I reached a point where we were frustrated and confused by all the different doctrines and ideas. He decided we should try a different approach, reading the Bible one book at a time, either in one sitting or at the very most in one day. This would give us a clearer understanding of all the questions above and help prevent taking verses or chapters out of context. I can tell you, this has been life-changing. I have heard of people opening their Bible to a random page, claiming it's the Spirit guiding them (in fact, I may have tried this once or twice myself :)), while I would say opening the Bible to a random page is better than letting it collect dust while you look at it guiltily, this can lead to much confusion unless the reader has

memorized the context of every verse in the Bible. 2
Timothy 2:15 says:

> *Study to shew thyself approved unto God, a
> workman that needeth not to be ashamed, rightly
> dividing the word of truth.*

I pray that this book, brings you revelations and
great change in your life towards a godlier motherhood and
home. Wherever you are in your journey and faith, I pray
your life is fruitful and shines a light upon God. In Jesus'
name, Amen!

PART 1

CHAPTER 1

Introduction and Purpose of This Book

Dear mothers of young ladies, You and I are Titus 2 Mothers. Perhaps we feel unable or underqualified for the role. Still, the repercussions of inaction, excuse-making, and self-righteousness often come all at once, like an unexpected slap in the face. If you're not paying attention, you won't be able to block the incoming hand. When it finally hits you (and it will), it hits hard, leaving a sting that has your mind reeling with 'Why?' and 'What did I do?' In the case of childrearing, the slap in the face is your children's character, their less-than-godly behaviors that seem to have crept in from nowhere. But the truth is, you forgot to put your guard up: you forgot to look at your child and, most importantly, yourself as an influence. We can look less at the 'What did I do?' and more at the 'What didn't I do?' and then 'What can I do to remedy this?' This inevitably involves a great deal of learning, change, and growth. I will be perfectly honest here and state my deficit in the motherhood department. However, my soul's goal is to grow into a biblical, godly mother. This desire has moved me to write this book. It is as much my journey as it is yours.

If this book is in your hands, I presume you are like me: in search of growth and godliness in motherhood, wifehood, and womanhood. We can find many of the answers we seek through biblical truth found in the book of Titus, Chapter 2. A Titus 2 Woman has the requisite character traits to train younger women in biblical, spirit-empowered, love-based living. This ideal woman only becomes possible through her godly demeanor. As a mother to a daughter, you want to be someone she can model, someone who is a positive presence in her life. We can be the light in the dark that guides them through the world, leading them toward a fruitful spirit. Ephesians 5:13 says:

But all things that are reproved are made manifest by the light: for whatsoever doth make manifest is light.

In order to embrace our roles and truly become them, we must have an understanding of the big picture and understand why we are becoming this Titus 2 Mother in the first place. The changes within ourselves will be profound, joyously fruitful, and gratefully bring us closer to God and other relationships. Here, I will journey through biblical encouragement with you, delving further into key phrases and what they look like within our lives. By putting on these godly characteristics, we can resist our fallen nature and grow into our true selves in Christ. We can become women who strengthen God's kingdom, glorifying God through our lives. But we must know, learn, and grow from a foundation of truth, the truth found in the Bible.

There is no reason why we cannot become these godly women. If we look around us at society, we can see a great amount of deception. Unfortunately, women tend to be the ones to fall for the lies and narratives parading as inclusive, tolerant, compassionate, and truthful. Society at large relies on the few to impact the many. Big change doesn't start with a surge of people but with everyday individuals standing up against tyranny and the crazy world before them, in declaration of the real truth, love, compassion, and grace. The seemingly insignificant individual becomes a catalyst for great change, prosperity, and freedom. We must be the ones to change. To stop this madness, the desecration of womanhood and family. We must give our husbands a worthy helper who is fruitful in everything she puts her hand to. This is our true service, our chance and opportunity to create real change within our world in a way that may, one day, have us face to face with the LORD, and the words 'Well done, my good and faithful servant' might greet our ears. That's what we all want to hear. Becoming a Titus 2 Mother might be the reason we hear those words.

TITUS CHAPTER 2

Let's take a look at Titus 2:

But speak thou the things which become sound doctrine: That the aged men be sober, grave, temperate, sound in faith, in charity, in patience. The aged women likewise, that they be in behaviour as becometh holiness, not false accusers, not given to much wine, teachers of good things; That they may teach the young women to be sober, to love their husbands, to love their children, To be discreet, chaste, keepers at home, good, obedient to their own husbands, that the word of God be not blasphemed. Young men likewise exhort to be sober minded. In all things shewing thyself a pattern of good works: in doctrine shewing uncorruptness, gravity, sincerity, Sound speech, that cannot be condemned; that he that is of the contrary part may be ashamed, having no evil thing to say of you. Exhort servants to be obedient unto their own masters, and to please them well in all things; not answering again; Not purloining, but shewing all good fidelity; that they may adorn the doctrine of God our Saviour in all things. For the grace of God that bringeth salvation hath appeared to all men, Teaching us that, denying ungodliness and worldly lusts, we should live soberly, righteously, and godly, in this present world; Looking for that blessed hope, and the glorious appearing of the great God and our Saviour Jesus Christ; Who gave himself for us, that he might redeem us from all iniquity, and purify unto himself a peculiar people, zealous of good works. These things speak, and exhort, and rebuke with all authority. Let no man despise thee.

Paul wrote to Titus, instructing him not to train the women in these Titus 2 qualities, but to call upon the older or "aged" women of the church who possess those desirable attributes mentioned, in order to teach the young women. In short, these older women are godly examples to the younger women. Most of us women are in search of such a role model all on our own; even in secular society, this is the case. In the secular community, a good, righteous role model is non-existent.

I was once very much a part of the broader world and culture, a subject of the fallen and twisted rhetoric of the devil. Before I came to faith, I surprisingly found myself looking to people like Ellie and Jared on YouTube and listening to Angie and Isaac Tolpin (Courageous Parenting). I only realized these people were Christian once I watched or listened to them for some time. (I am unsure how this happened as they mention Jesus and Christianity a lot – I guess you hear what you want to hear). I also found myself liking curriculums for homeschooling that happened to be foundational in Christian values. I found myself frustrated due to the lack of my own faith, annoyed that I aligned with so much of what these people spoke of and what these curriculums encouraged but didn't accept the God they preached. Stubbornness eventually gave way to love, and I came to the Father on my knees with a sob and a thankful heart. It had been many years of praying in secret, asking believers why they believed, and spending time in contemplation. Never in that time had I picked up the Bible and read. That was when life changed forever: reading the Bible. Reading the historical events that I had been told were made-up baloney, and realizing and feeling the truth behind every story, event, and parable. The truth of our

Savior Jesus and the beautiful gift given by our God was heartwarming and transformational. I felt my heart become flesh (EZE 36:26). Watching the world's darkness unfold helped, it showed how much the light, the good, and the righteous are needed. It made me long for love, warmth, and comfort from something beyond myself, something that actually made sense.

Before I came to the faith, life seemed unbearable. My husband was at work, and my baby was tottering around, learning the art of walking and speech. I was buried under a pile of hand-me-down clothes, furniture, and more. We never had much money, so well-meaning people often gave us things they no longer wanted, turning our home into a collection of op-shop, mismatched bits and bobs. Our home looked like a closing-down charity shop. I'd spend much of my time researching and looking for solutions to turn our crap heap into a homely home. I found many fads and movements to take on and essentially idolize as I attempted to become the woman who advocated for these different ideas and ideals in life and home living. Things like zero waste and minimalism: ridding oneself of any extras and unnecessary possessions. The thing is, life is complicated and forever changing. What you enjoy and spend your time doing today may be different tomorrow or even a year from now. Ridding yourself of stuff won't necessarily fix anything, especially when other people live in your household with very different ideas of lifestyle and living. It's easy to fall for the lies told by 'gurus' when you're being told you will be happy if only: "insert slogan here." The true solution was knowing when to say no, having self-control, and feeling content enough to know we didn't need more. This was a notion we eventually worked out. It seems simple now, but it took several years to learn. It would have been better if we'd had this leadership to guide us in our decision-making earlier. Coming to faith has, in many ways, rectified this issue, and now we look to God and His Word for guidance. We all need leadership – not just any leadership, but godly leadership.

DEFINING A TITUS 2 WOMAN

Pastors are meant to be the godly leaders of the church; they possess vast responsibilities within their congregation. But a pastor cannot do it all on his own. Delegation: having a leadership structure is necessary for having an organized church. You need the right people for the right jobs, and so having the pastor select godly aged women (hereafter called the Titus 2 Woman) to be the primary role models for the younger women of the community could prove to be much more fruitful than the alternative, younger women choosing their own exemplars. With that in mind, it's important to remember that we often have many influences outside the congregation, whether we wish to or not, for better or worse. Paul's guidance helps to ensure some godly role models are in the mix.

We can understand this need for delegation and a leadership structure because it's the same within a home: The father is the head of the household, the wife is under him, and the children are under her. We can delegate to older children or our husbands. We can even get outside help if necessary – and sometimes it truly is essential – but there lies the biggest task; knowing when to delegate, knowing when the obstacle is far too grand for one person alone. God's Word gives us many instances of leadership structure, and these are things we must utilize to maintain some sense of order and structure within our homes. One of the biggest problems we face is pastors favoring political jargon and worldly ways instead of focusing on the biblical leadership found in the Bible, like the teachings in Titus.

Paul details how these Titus 2 Women should be so that they can be good, godly role models for younger women. To be a Titus 2 Woman, she is supposed to be a woman who has raised her children biblically (who have since grown and moved out of home), has been on her journey of growth, is consistent in godly character and has an exemplary relationship with her husband. The problem today is not just a lack of pastoral interest in selecting such women to guide the younger, but the lack of these Titus 2 Women existing in the first place. We are in the fallen world, and it has continued to suck in even the most intellectual or 'wise' women, with the devil parading numerous unbiblical narratives as righteous when they are a violation that goes against our very being and design. Therefore, I am stressing the need for us to embody the Titus 2 Woman, by becoming a Titus 2 Mother, and take on these characteristics now.

We must become Titus 2 Mothers for our daughters, who desperately require a Titus 2 Woman in their lives. We are their example of how to live as a woman in the world and not of the world. A Titus 2 Woman is needed in the community, but a Titus 2 Mother is needed in the home. Our minds must be focused on Christ and His sacrifice so we can serve from a place of love, joy, and peace. John 16:33 says:

> *These things I have spoken unto you, that in me ye might have peace. In the world ye shall have tribulation: but be of good cheer; I have overcome the world.*

Becoming a Titus 2 Mother will enable us to drop the distractions around us and truly listen to His word. Do you fit the description of a Titus 2 Woman? Most of us will say 'no'; this is a good thing, for now, we shall see the glory of God within us and our lives when we listen, study, and enact all these things, which Titus 2 mentions, as it is profitable for doctrine, for reproof, for correction, and for instruction in righteousness (2 TIM 3:16).

Now, come with me to delve deeper into the meaning behind Titus 2. We'll break down what it truly means by using a wide range of biblical references to better understand our role as mothers and women of influence in God's kingdom...

Take Aways

- A war has been waged against us by Satan, and it's up to us to stand steadfast in faith and fight with all the spiritual tools we have and develop those we don't to glorify God.
- The Bible contains all the teachings needed to become a Titus 2 Woman. We need only study and read to learn and grow from the great gift God has given us: His word.

Heart Probing Questions

1. What kind of mother do you want to be?
2. Are you always acting with Jesus in your heart and mind?
3. What fruit are your children showing, if any? Why or why not?
4. What do you feel you need to work on the most within your home and mothering?

CHAPTER 2

The Humble Priestess

I often consider my home to be a church. It is a place where my believing family congregates, where we teach, speak, and share God's word. In my home, my husband is the pastor, I am the Titus 2 Mother, and my daughter is the 'younger woman' of Titus 2. It's incredible how much a child soaks in their surroundings, even when they seem like they're not paying attention. They are! Their brain is forming pathways and connections that may, later down the track, shock you or send you into a frenzy of 'Why?' and 'Where did they learn this from?' Most of the time, the answer you seek comes *back* to you or your husband. You're the role models. You set the tone. You set the guidelines of what is and isn't acceptable. A church pastor should be a spiritual leader and an example of how to live. He is supposed to be a living example of God's teachings. Of course, the pastor, like you, is still human and not infallible, but as a teacher, his bar must be higher, as must yours as a teacher to your child. Paul, in Titus 2:3, states that the Titus 2 Woman is to be like a holy priest, serving in the presence of God and leading the younger women in their faith and worship. Here, the Titus 2 Mother becomes a priestess in the home, shining a light to the LORD within her home-centered ministry. This Titus 2 Mother Priestess is a powerhouse when coupled with her Leading Pastor Husband.

THE PICTURE OF HOUSEWIVES

Picture yourself as the Titus 2 Mother, the priestess of your home. What do you look like, act like, and talk like? What does your home look and feel like? I know that God's word tells us to be content (PHI 4:11-13), but being content with yourself doesn't mean you don't aspire to be more or better than you currently are. With the social media culture today, it can be hard to picture an image we haven't already seen: the ideal kitchen in the country-style home, pristine with a hint of shabby chic and a touch of Hampton beach house; images of forever smiling faces with the perfect attire (think 50s' housewives). But this is not necessarily reality or the reality God has ordained for you. When we cling to imagery and ideals, they can quickly become idols. We become like those in the book of Amos singing praise to God without feeling the words in our hearts (AMO 6:5). We become like The Stepford Wives, robotically doing the daily things for a beautiful home without looking to glorify God or even consider Him in thought or service.

Here, I must warn you not to look enviously at others (PRO 14:30), wanting what they have. God didn't create us to be the same. We are made differently, with a unique mix of characteristics, drives, and abilities. If we focus on others and not our service to God, letting the sin of envy overtake our true calling to serve the LORD, we play into the enemy's hands and leave ourselves open to ridicule, deceit, and discontent. You have two choices. You can either let the world shape you or take a different approach, one of diligent study (PRO 11:27), persistent faith (GAL 6:9), and self-control (JAS 1:12), with a focus on the LORD our God. You are called to change and take action while still using the mind God has given you (2 TIM 1:7). 2 Peter 1:5-8 says:

> *And beside this, giving all diligence, add to your faith virtue; and to virtue knowledge; And to knowledge temperance; and to temperance patience; and to patience godliness; And to godliness*

brotherly kindness; and to brotherly kindness charity. For if these things be in you, and abound, they make you that ye shall neither be barren nor unfruitful in the knowledge of our Lord Jesus Christ.

We must think ahead, learn, grow, and change as our family requires. We cannot be idle and expect fruitful change to occur. Fruitful change is a result of good intent followed by action. Our intentions ultimately need to be driving us toward Christ. As the priestess of our home, our actions and teachings are to be in service of Him. This allows us to serve our family and others in the unique way God has created us. How do we keep our minds focused? God has given us an answer in Philippians 4:8:

Finally, brethren, whatsoever things are true, whatsoever things are honest, whatsoever things are just, whatsoever things are pure, whatsoever things are lovely, whatsoever things are of good report; if there be any virtue, and if there be any praise, think on these things.

I will be honest. I find myself easily swayed by what is around me. In true Eve fashion, I – like many other women – am inclined to be deceived in that vulnerable nature. I find that what I see and listen to has a significant effect on me, to the point where I now rarely watch or listen to any secular content. I can give a genuinely horrifying example of what kind of effect the wrong viewing can have on one's psyche. I was a teen living partly with my boyfriend, now husband, and I was up late waiting for him to return home from work. I decided to watch Wuthering Heights, a supposed classic film worthy of my time, only it wasn't. It caught me in a whirlwind of darkness, and I sank low into the pit of despair, almost feeling as if I were the main character, Kathy. I was completely submerged in my viewing experience. When Sebastian returned home, he found me in an emotionally catatonic state. He asked me what was wrong and saw what I was watching, the film now nearing its end. Wisely, he switched it off and told me never to watch it again. He held me and had me breathe slowly. I admit, at the time, I was in darkness as it was. Childhood wasn't the best experience for me, and adolescence was certainly unforgiving regarding the effects on my character and well-being. Even so, surely a film shouldn't have the power to send someone into emotional turmoil. But it can. This experience is one of many I have had personally. We are made to connect through stories – historically, humanity has always connected generations through storytelling and re-telling past events. We cannot be so prideful as to think we are not affected by what we view and see on a screen. Just because our conscious mind knows it isn't real doesn't mean it won't affect our subconscious or have us reliving moments in time through a jogging of memory.

SACRIFICIAL LIFE

Before faith, I was an avid viewer of films, TV shows, and day-in-the-life videos on YouTube, not always paying attention to the changes occurring in my character and life. I was naïve and blinded by the so-called 'viewing pleasure' I was getting from numbing out to the blah in front of me. Since coming to faith, I have been trying to instead avoid TV altogether unless it is non-fiction or something to build my skills in the home or my aspirations. This is a suitable method for those of us who find ourselves easily influenced. It keeps us focused on tasks and growing in both character and skill. It also shows our children our self-discipline and self-control in even the seemingly small things. Of course, it helps to have a supportive husband in this; God has blessed me with a husband who protects me and encourages me not to dwell on what pulls me toward the ungodly but what is good and right to the LORD. He reminds me that if we ask the LORD for guidance in faith, we will be on the right path to learning the necessary skills to fulfill our purpose. Orienting our lives through faith helps us to serve the LORD in love. When we are focused on God, we act with more integrity, goodness, and righteousness. This behavior glorifies the LORD as it shows our sacred personal devotion to God and how that influences every aspect of our lives. Romans 12:1-2 says:

I beseech you therefore, brethren, by the mercies of God, that ye present your bodies a living sacrifice, holy, acceptable unto God, which is your reasonable service. And be not conformed to this world: but be ye transformed by the renewal of your mind, that ye may prove what is that good, and acceptable and perfect, will of God.

As Christians, not just women and mothers, we should exalt God in opposition to the world and perform various duties respecting God, ourselves, and others. To the best of our ability, we should present our lives as living sacrifices to the LORD, just as he sacrificed himself for us. This is our reasonable service to God. As priestesses, we can remind ourselves of what is truly important: John 3:16 says:

For God so loved the world, that he gave his only begotten son, that whosoever believeth in him should not perish, but have everlasting life.

Jesus died for us so that we could live. That very sacrifice is why we must live as priestesses, looking to the LORD and asking for His guidance. We have been saved by His grace. As mothers, many of us already understand this sacrificial life in a physical sense when we sacrifice our bodies in the name of family and procreation. When our tummy stretches and becomes unrecognizable, our bodies almost no longer feel like our own. But the truth is, we are not our own, as 1 Corinthians 6:19-20 says:

> *What? know ye not that your body is the temple of the Holy Ghost which is in you, which ye have of God, and ye are not your own? For ye are bought with a price: therefore glorify God in your body, and in your spirit, which are God's.*

We have been bought at a price through the blood and sacrifice of Jesus Christ, and we must be willing in this. Through our faith, we become a temple (dwelling place) for the Holy Spirit, which is of God. We have duties in this sacrificial life, our worship through our physical, intentional, and spiritual presence having been moved by the mercy and goodness of God. We have been exhorted to sobriety and humility by recognizing our gifts as God-given (ROM 12); we can increase our desire to do what we should through our faith, obedience, and discipline. Our most significant duty of all is put eloquently in Galatians 2:20, which says:

> *I am crucified with Christ: nevertheless, I live; yet am not I, but Christ liveth in me: and the life which I now live in the flesh I live by the faith of the Son of God, who loved me, and gave himself me.*

We give ourselves (mind, body, and soul) to God, and through doing so, we become a testament to our faith and a shining light toward God, glorifying His goodness. This is something we want to do for our daughters. We want to raise them in Christ so they might stay with Him into adulthood and beyond. God calls us to have children painfully (GEN 3:16), but He also tells us they are to be brought up faithful, not accused of rioting or unruly behaviors (TIT 1:6). So in that, we understand that we are not just to have children but bring them up knowing the LORD and loving Him, seeing His works through us and others, so they might build a steadfast, and incorruptible faith. Our daughters are our most sacred task as mothers, as we are their first female influence, and we show them what is good and acceptable to the LORD. We have all heard the saying, 'Like mother, like daughter.' We can find this sentiment in Ezekiel 16:44:

> *Behold, every one that useth proverbs shall use this proverb against thee, saying, as is the mother, as is her daughter.*

Sass Equals Sass

My husband can find babies challenging; their noises and tickly fingers work to annoy him. It's sometimes unreasonable, for sure, but so too has been my reaction to his on occasion. If I heard him getting irritated, I too would get annoyed and tell him harshly to "calm down" or that there was "no need for his attitude," that "our son is only a baby," and to "work on being less annoyed!" He always agreed with me, but my approach to the situation created animosity inside me. As my husband's irate behavior lessened, mine continued to be more animated. One day, after first reading Titus 2, I made a discernible effort to hold my tongue, knowing that I needed to be grateful and loving to my husband and discuss necessary issues when the children were out of earshot. Otherwise, we were not showing a united front. This was when I saw my daughter saying what I had been saying to her father, with more sass and feeling than I remember putting into words. There was disrespect and self-righteousness all over her face and within her words – my words. I heard them, and I knew them; my husband hadn't entirely caught on, but he didn't appreciate our daughter's attitude. I was horrified, realizing I had caused this. I had trained my daughter how to disrespect and be self-righteous. It was awful to realize but also a blessing.

We have a clear teaching in Ezekiel 16:44 that our daughters reflect our personality and behavior; traits and features are inherited. This may bring on fear and recollections of past events. Here, we see our true impact as the Titus 2 Mother Priestess and what a lack of humility and self-control within ourselves does to our child. Our influence, be it good or bad, is copied and re-enacted like a

TV series where the main character is swapped out for a newer, younger model, only the older cast member is still on set watching from the sidelines, exposed to all that they had done in the show through the poorly acted replacement that everyone says is just like the original. Because of the influence we have on our daughters, we must do our due diligence and make sure that the example we set will grow character and enhance the LORD'S kingdom, not dismantle it. We mustn't dwell on past actions but focus on what we can do now to rectify behaviors that have grown in our wake. So, how do we guide our daughters in the way they should go (PRO 22:6)? We must be calm and remember we are not alone: we have God (JOS 1:9), and we have all that we need in His word (2 TIM 3:16). Jesus in Matthew 18:20 says:

> *For where two or three are gathered together in my name, there am I in the midst of them.*

When we teach our children with the love of Christ in our hearts, and we teach them about Him, He is with us. As the Titus 2 Mother Priestess, it's important not to panic or fret about what to do but rather calmly ask God for the guidance, clarity, and patience needed to make a change. God has given us the guidelines with which we can teach and teach well, within the Bible. Our tasks as humble priestesses are to look, study, and understand that God has entrusted us with this position. He is good, righteous, and all-knowing. Whether we can see it or not, there is a reason for our position and for each specific child. We can apologize to our daughters for wrongdoing or wrong teachings and then tell them about the journey we are embarking on to be better mothers. We can express how much we want to do a good job and how we will work hard to teach them all the right things through the Holy Spirit and the LORD. This is us showing humility and shining a light to God. His influence changes us, and our hearts become flesh (EZE 36:26) so we can love deeper, connect, and bring His sons and daughters to Him and away from the darkness. As the priestess of the home, just like a pastor in the church, we must be aware of the many obstacles that the enemy leaves in his wake. Obstacles that are there to trip us up, corrupt us, and lead us into a pit of despair or unbelief. There are ways to safeguard ourselves against these attacks. God has outlined the tools we need and how we might best use them. We need only to look…

TAKE AWAYS

- You are the priestess of your home. You guide your children spiritually alongside your husband. If you are not doing as you should, your children will be affected.
- There are character traits that a priestess should embody: self-control and humility.
- It would help if you talked to your children about the journey you are embarking on and how you hope it will affect your life as well as theirs.

HEART PROBING QUESTIONS

1. Do you feel you are acting as the priestess in your home? Why or why not?
2. Have you at any time undermined your husband's authority or disciplinary methods? Why or why not? How might you rectify this?
3. How might you approach this Titus 2 Mother subject with your children?

CHAPTER 3

Guarded Speech

Y ou can imagine that when one is feeling emotional, words can spill out—erupting like a dormant volcano, covering itself and the village below in chaos, destroying all that is around it. Words can be a dagger to the heart and a mighty sword to the soul, penetrating all that is good and holy. The problem with words is their power within our world. A word can make a person believe evil of themselves or others, dehumanizing us, creations of God. We see this in the 'blue eyes/brown eyes exercise.' Jane Elliott, an educator in 1968, was prompted by the death of civil rights leader Martin Luther King Jr. and first conducted the anti-racism experiment in her all-white third-grade classroom the day after Jr.'s death. The children in the class were told that the blue-eyed children were superior and the brown-eyed children were inferior.

The classroom experiment mirrored what was witnessed in WW2, where Hitler and the Nazi party told all the German people that the Jews were lesser, inferior, disease-carrying, inhuman beings, and the rest of the German populace were superior, clean, and disease-free. In the experiment, Elliott found that the superior blue-eyed children treated the inferior brown-eyed children as lesser. This sentiment was shown in their work and test scores, and their grades were indicative of their superior or inferior nature. A nature that had been shaped using words through the influence of their teacher. On the second day of the experiment, the same group of children were then told the opposite was true. She used examples to prove to the children that she had lied to them and that the brown-eyed children were the truly superior ones, while blue-eyed children were inferior; she used examples like a blue-eyed student leaving their glasses at home as proof of their inferiority. The very same results occurred: the inferior behaved inferiorly, and the superior behaved superiorly. Mrs. Elliott then completed the experiment she conducted in a few days with a discussion. The children were asked thought-provoking questions about how the experiment made them feel and what they had learned about fairness and judging people. In the end, Elliott used her questions to lead the children to understand that we should never judge a person based on the color of their eyes or skin, as these things don't indicate intelligence or personality. Similar exercises have been conducted in prisons and other classrooms, some with mixed nationalities and ages.

These experiments can quickly get out of hand, snowballing into violence, and can prove fatal for unlucky participants. WW2 shows us the influence words have and the horrors that can follow. Millions have died because millions more believed them to be less than human. As Titus 2 Mother Priestesses, we must filter our words and ensure that what we say is good and God-glorifying. In the previous chapter, I mentioned that our children are like sponges soaking in everything we do and say. Well, let me tell you, one day, that sponge will start dripping or be rung out, and when it happens, you don't want to be horrified by the results. Results that you cultivated. We help create these undesirable traits in our children by setting the wrong example. We ordain these results through our modeling of the same or similar undesirable actions prior to their emulation. We set the stage and the example of what is right and acceptable within our society, home, and culture. God shows us that the Word was what formed creation. Words are there for us to build His kingdom. To understand the extent of this truth, we could look to the book of Genesis, but let's look to John 1:1 instead and what he eloquently says about the word:

> In the beginning there was the Word, and the Word was with God, and the Word was God.

Our world was created by God and His Word, and just as the written word is God speaking to us, we can see God's writing in creation itself, right down to the binary information encoded in our genes. With this in mind, it's no surprise that Satan would deceive us into using language for evil, not good. We can all recall a time when we have said something we regret or must apologize for later. We have all messed up at one time or another when we were in a season that had us frazzled and fatigued with responsibility and duty.

ARGUMENTS WITH OUR HUSBANDS

Paul writes to Titus 2 Women not to be "false accusers." If we break this down and think on the real-world moments of this, even on a tiny scale, we gain a better understanding of why he felt the need to write it. It is often said in jest that women remember everything, and more specifically, everything bad their husband has done, especially in an argument. I feel the reason he states for women not to be 'false accusers' instead of liars is because when we recall events and moments, we do so through emotion, and emotions can cloud judgments and change details. Past events can be distorted in our minds through our emotional state. When we are confidently stating a distorted reality, we are not attempting to deceive. We believe what we are saying is true. A liar is someone who intentionally tells a falsehood, not someone who believes what they are saying is true. From my own perspective, "false accusers" prompts me not just to speak of what I believe to be true but to think long and hard about what I am saying, why I am saying it, and who I am saying it to.

Emotionally, in an argument, we want to say something to fight back, but we harm our desire for God and the Holy Spirit in defending our pride. Our words are cannon fodder, used for the enemy's gain and our loss. I can recall countless arguments before faith where my husband "shockingly" told me I remembered something wrong, that my account of events was untrue, and that I was a liar. It hurt, I remember constantly feeling even angrier, misunderstood, underappreciated, and worthless. The devil wants this: strife and discontent between husband and wife.

We see this evil at work in society, with the annihilation and breakdown of the family unit through the destruction of the mother-and-father relationship. The rhetoric regarding family, depicted on TV, in books, throughout education, and within organizations, caters and programs to meet the secular narrative-friendly requirements: family is unimportant, children are a burden, parents are silly and don't understand, love yourself, focus on self-care and being happy. The prevalent use of derogatory words and phrases to mock and down-grade family and gender collide in a mishmash, telling us that our God-ordained and designed roles are nothing more than societal constructs, depriving us of self-satisfaction and desire. I have regrettably played into the mockery, saying phrases like 'silly daddy' and allowing teasing to go on in my own home, either by myself, my children, my husband, or other family members. This small but persistent banter may seem harmless, but over time, it can chip away at our husband's self-esteem and personal beliefs, negatively affecting his ability to lead. Here, we can draw parallels between our effect on our husbands and the "blue-eye, brown-eye" experiment's effects on the children, especially the negative impact on those treated as inferior. Our tongues may be small, but they can have a profoundly significant impact on ourselves and others. James 3:5-18 warns us of this saying:

> *Even so the tongue is a little member, and boasteth great things. Behold, how great a matter a little fire kindleth! And the tongue is a fire, a world of iniquity: so is the tongue among our members, that it defileth the whole body, and setteth on fire the*

course of nature; and it is set on fire of hell. For every kind of beasts, and of birds, and of serpents, and of things in the sea, is tamed, and hath been tamed of mankind: But the tongue can no man tame; it is an unruly evil, full of deadly poison. Therewith bless we God, even the Father; and therewith curse we men, which are made after the similitude of God. Out of the same mouth proceedeth blessing and cursing. My brethren, these things ought not so to be. Doth a fountain send forth at the same place sweet water and bitter? Can the fig tree, my brethren, bear olive berries? either a vine, figs? so can no fountain both yield salt water and fresh. Who is a wise man and endued with knowledge among you? let him shew out of a good conversation his works with meekness of wisdom. But if ye have bitter envying and strife in your hearts, glory not, and lie not against the truth. This wisdom descendeth not from above, but is earthly, sensual, devilish. For where envying and strife is, there is confusion and every evil work. But the wisdom that is from above is first pure, then peaceable, gentle, and easy to be intreated, full of mercy and good fruits, without partiality, and without hypocrisy. And the fruit of righteousness is sown in peace of them that make peace.

GOSSIP AND OTHER FORMS OF HARMFUL SPEECH

The tongue is a small part of us, but the problems that arise from its improper use can quickly descend into chaos. James describes the working of the tongue: it can be used for both good and evil, and it can be a shining light to God or a tool for the devil. Christians are tasked with growing in faith and saving our words for truth. Let's take a look at a quote that is more explicitly aimed at wives. 1 Timothy 3:11:

> *Even so must their wives be grave, not slanderers, sober, faithful in all things.*

Though we all have this issue of the tongue, both men and women, women are regularly targeted with this correction. It is well known that women like to chat. We're good at communicating with others and connecting with people emotionally, as generally, we possess more of a capacity for compassion. The problem with this ability to converse is that it can often become tainted in the form of speech named gossip. Gossip can sometimes start from humble and seemingly harmless beginnings yet end harmfully or maliciously. Even the purest of hearts speaking of others result in sharing sensitive, private information, harming someone's perceived character and/or their ministry. It is clear why women are targeted in Paul's warning because, historically, we are the ones most easily deceived and manipulated. This is discussed in 1 Timothy 2:11-14, which gives us the remedy for our shortfall as well, saying:

> *Let the woman learn in silence with all subjection. But I suffer not a woman to teach, nor to usurp authority over the man, but to be in silence. For Adam was first formed, then Eve. And Adam was not deceived, but the woman being deceived was in the transgression.*

He goes all the way back and mentions the first man and woman and how a man's authority over a woman began with Adam and Eve. Paul brought this up because it exemplifies women's involvement in being deceived. He states that a woman should silently learn and not usurp authority over a man. Let's take this to the home where the husband is the Pastor, and we are the Titus 2 Mother. We understand that as mothers and teachers of our children, it would first be wise to receive our husband's counsel for clarity and understanding so we are not deceived or teaching incorrectly. I will also mention that this doesn't mean that we are to always go along with our husbands when what he is doing is against God. The Bible shows us instances where women have stepped forward, occasionally resisting their husbands' authority, which was a good thing. In Esther, she fasted for three days (EST 4:16) before going to the king, her husband, to ask him to save her people, the Jews, from being slaughtered in his name. Her husband, the king, obliged her and found a way to protect her people. He did this even though she came to him without a summons, which was against the law – his law. She was led by God, but her husband was led by the evil Haman. The Bible can be an intricate tool filled with many examples of how and how not to use words. In the case of Sapphira (ACT 5:1-11), she went along with her husband and his lie; only the lie was against God, which caused both of them to die, one after another. She could have saved herself had she been truthful. We get a clear message and lesson to use the brains we have been given so we might know when we need to resist and when we need to obey. Spending time in prayer and the word through faith will ensure that we are focused on God and his design for us. Paul's teaching in 1 Timothy 2:11 only works when both husband and wife are active participants in the fulfillment of our creator's design.

I have occasionally undermined my husband's authority, mainly before faith, where I had belittled, joked about, or ignored something he had asked the children or me to do. In any polite conversation, this is, of course, no good, but we all too often become sinfully comfortable in our own homes and regress into our fallen nature, allowing the devil to play his tricks, parading them as fun and playful banter, when all they do is fuel a fire that is all discontent, anguish, and pain. I have improved dramatically in this area but still occasionally fall prey to the enemy and say something mockingly or in thoughtless disregard. Society tells us: 'You don't need a man to complete you,' and 'You can make your own way, girl!' and 'Don't let him tell you what to do,' but that is not God's design for us, which Paul mentions.

An Example of the Holy Spirit

We must disregard the sentiments of society and instead inherit a godly mindset and vocabulary that has us thinking about and choosing our words carefully to serve our husbands, which ultimately serves the LORD who designed the male-and-female partnership that way. We model this God's design to our children. Make no mistake; you are modeling this for better or worse. I can humble myself and say we were most certainly modeling for the worse before faith, and now I feel that the children get to see the Holy Spirit in action as we improve and grow over time. My oldest has seen the changes, and his faith seems strong and steadfast. He is old enough to remember what we were like before and after faith, so he has the ability to make a clear comparison. We, on occasion, argue in front of the children, causing a scene and a palpable atmosphere within the home that is uncomfortable and uninviting. This is where we take a punch to the ego and talk to our children, telling them that God is helping us and that we want to be better parents and not argue. We explain our non-religious roots and how a childhood without faith set us on this sinful path that takes work and self-control to get out of. Sharing this with our children can become a testimony of God's wonders, strengthening their faith and hearts. I'll be honest: it can be confronting and scary, especially when your child's unfiltered and unapologetic response confirms the faults you have described and gives further examples, but it's a good, humbling experience and one of growth and a more profound connection with your child. They learn they can come to you no matter what, even when it's about your shortfalls. Our children have even prayed for us to have God's help in being better parents and not fighting, which was heart-*breaking* and warming at the same time. This is an excellent show of how our words at the moment are just as important as our words for the future. Our wants and dreams to be what God ordains, and our show that we all sin, impact our children here and now. It is how we approach our sinful behavior that matters; therefore, it is good to make our faith visible in the home so that by the spirit we should model godliness to our children.

The very real thing we must remember is what James 3:5-18 states: The tongue can be the devil's tool and we are his favorite weapon to use against God. Therefore, we must use our mind, teachable heart, and, most

importantly, obedience to God and our husbands (EPH
5:22-33) to help us walk with God and lead our children by
example. But how can we when we are bombarded daily by
sin, when the very fabric of womanhood, motherhood, and
wifehood is being frayed, and slowly, each thread is being
pulled away? Sadly, in our world today, deception is all
around us, even to the point where much of what I have
already said is triggering for some women.

FEMINIST BRAINWASHING

The feminist movement has decimated our God-
given roles and formed a wedge between husbands and
wives, telling them that they are equally leading and neither
needs to be submissive to the other. This sentiment isn't just
taught to adults but to unsuspecting children, brainwashing
them from a young age. Society at large teaches our
children and us that men and women should focus on
pursuing self-satisfaction, self-fulfillment, and happiness.
This may sound good from the outside, but a life focused
only on 'self' is one of empty and selfish desires. Jesus, by
contrast, showed us a life of service and sacrifice. The
opinion cultivated through the predominant education
system of our time advocates for a life free of the restraints
that accompany motherhood and wifehood, and the solution
to all that ails these contemporary women is to step out of

the repressive clutches of a patriarchal world and step forth into a homogenous utopia.

Let's face it. We're not headed toward a utopia but a destructive nightmare where gender is meaningless. The homogeneity of the marriage relationship is like a play with two equal, headstrong directors: how can both lead in their own ways to create the same play? The answer is they can't. We are unique, and often, we can become prideful and self-righteous. The play with two headstrong directors has several possible outcomes: it's never created, it's a mess, or someone takes the dominant role, and the other director becomes more of an assistant director. If this isn't the case and both directors really do have an equal voice, there would need to be a mediator to solve disputes, who would ultimately have the final say, thus serving as the head. In the rare case that two people have the same will regarding a broader project, the likelihood of perfect agreement on further projects and on nuances that arise from longer-term ventures will continually decrease. This is because of the increased amount and variation of points of agreement over time. If there is to be any congruency over the long term, two people can't have an equal place in leadership over the same things. There will have to be much compromise and a final say.

God's design was for man to be the head of the family. He's the leader, the one who is not easily deceived.

The wife is under him, under his protection, so that she may not be deceived even when the devil is out for her. God's word teaches us that children are a blessing and that a union between man and woman is a sacred partnership, equally necessary and accepted by both participants. A married woman is to willingly submit herself to her husband and deliver new, light-filled life into the world. A married man, in marriage, is to uphold his faith and connection to God and protect his family from evil through exemplary leadership. We have been made for a specific purpose. A woman cannot do the role of a man. Likewise, a man cannot take the role of a woman. This is what we need our children to know in order to prepare them against the lies of the world.

FEMINISM AND ABORTION

Our words are important and must be guarded, especially as women who have been deceived and, in many cases, are vulnerable to falling prey to deception again. Women are being used as tools in the devil's game: to bring about death, destruction, and an unholiness that will transcend generations. Feminist groups catch women with phrases like 'my body, my choice,' but the very spearheads of the movements and organizations often are, or were, eugenics enthusiasts and advocates. Margaret Sanger, the founder of Planned Parenthood, presented herself as an ally to all women, but most women are unaware of her beliefs. Margaret Sanger was a known eugenics and Ku Klux Klan advocate. She coined the term birth control, which was one of her most significant achievements. She wanted mass attainability and affordability, hoping to render those she deemed unfit or unworthy of breeding within society unable to have children. The main groups she targeted for population control were blacks, Jews, slaves, and Italians. You see, she was an extremely racist woman who believed the black or 'negro' community were lesser beings, needing to be bred/weeded out. In "The Pivot of Civilization" and "A Plan for Peace," Sanger explains the benefits of eliminating these persons through eugenics:

Our failure to segregate morons who are increasing and multiplying ... demonstrates our foolhardy and extravagant sentimentalism ...

[Philanthropists] encourage the healthier and more normal sections of the world to shoulder the burden of unthinking and indiscriminate fecundity of others; which brings with it, as I think the reader must agree, a dead weight of human waste. Instead of decreasing and aiming to eliminate the stocks that are most detrimental to the future of the race and the world, it tends to render them to a menacing degree dominant ...

We are paying for, and even submitting to, the dictates of an ever-increasing, unceasingly spawning class of human beings who never should have been born at all.

The main object of the Population Congress would be: ... to apply a stern and rigid policy of sterilization and segregation to that grade of population whose progeny is tainted or whose inheritance is such that objectionable traits may be transmitted to offspring... to give certain dysgenic groups in our population their choice of segregation or sterilization.

So, you see, this whole birth control monster started on the back of racism and disguised itself as a freedom movement. Sanger was an unstoppable, evil machine, advocating for systems at a government level. In 1934, she told America Weekly that the idea was that if someone wanted children, they would first have to submit a request. This request would then be viewed, accepted, or declined based on what would 'benefit society.' Those lucky few who were granted permission would be given some kind of birth permit. Imagine that: a permit to have a child.

There is a misconception that Planned Parenthood has changed and detached itself from its racist, anti-Semitic, and eugenicist roots. However, this is untrue. 'Planned

Parenthood' was originally the 'American Birth Control League.' Sanger changed the name due to her less-than-favorable acknowledgments and praise of Hitler during WW2. She publicly praised his politically fueled eugenics program. When WW2 ended, she didn't want to be associated with a man the world hated. So Planned Parenthood was born. After the name change, Planned Parenthood advocated for the Chinese Government's policy to force women to have abortions against their will. They also advocated for the sterilization of the third world. Since Sanger died in 1966, her successors have praised her work, including Faye Wattleton:

> *As we celebrate the 100th birthday of Margaret Sanger, our courageous leader, we should be very proud of what we are and what our mission is. It is a very grand mission; abortion is only the tip of the iceberg.*

You may need a check-up if that speech doesn't send a chill down your spine. The saddest thing now is that the government – in other words, the taxpayer, you – also pays for the annihilation of these babies through the hundreds of millions of dollars given to the organization each year. Abortion, since its inception, has become a routine operation, happening over 73 million times a year. Imagine that 73 million children are slaughtered yearly in the name of freedom and self-righteousness. It's truths like this that should have us reeling and moved to action so we can speak truth into the world and light up the path toward God. This is where parenting comes in. We can educate and equip our children with this knowledge. It's horrible to think of and discuss, but necessary in a world that can distort and manipulate the truth to look like lies. We must equip our children with the knowledge of this evil so they can be strengthened in faith and stand steadfast in this fight against murder.

SOCIAL MEDIA

As Christian women, we must see through the lies. Only then can we arm ourselves with truth through diligent study and research. Looking into truths, like the roots and history of Planned Parenthood and the wickedly evil Margaret Sanger, is necessary. Our daughters require this from us: the techniques and ways to research and learn the truth that we find become tools for our children. Our daughters learn not just from our knowledge; once equipped, they can also build their own. We must equip them in this online arena as much as we do in the physical world. They need to know when to speak their minds or hold their tongues. They need to know when to consult with their husbands, family, or church and when they are required to face something alone. We need our daughters to value having a deeper understanding of a situation or event before speaking of it. Only then can we prevent the word vomit so many feel encouraged to speak these days.

The biggest problem today is the ease with which we are all able to 'speak our minds' and spread propaganda rhetoric. With our minds usually full of pride, in search of glorification, we turn to one of many applications on one of our many devices and create a post that, in many cases, is likely to be spread and shared quickly and, dependent on content, could destroy lives, friendships, and businesses in an instant. Personal beliefs, politics, and anything of substance and meaning become trivialized. Many individuals and groups find themselves in echo chambers, making little to no difference in the world yet having the illusion of making a difference. That's how the devil wants us, thinking we are changing things, thinking we are active in making a difference when we are alienating people and adding to the lies and confusion.

A great example of this is the division caused by COVID-19. From closed shop windows and doors plastered in signage to empty patronage seen inside and absent family members at gatherings or your own missed invitation. Divisiveness can be seen everywhere. I fell prey to the devil's game, finding myself caught in a cycle of fear and stress. I watched the world descend into darkness, or at least that's how it felt from the keyboard end of what was becoming my reality. My posts on social media were divisive, emotional, frantic, and downright devilish. They stirred the pot and caused havoc wherever they went. I thought of my daughter posting how I did, and it left a foul taste in my mouth. I want my daughter to be able to articulate herself in a way that is edifying for others. It took time, but eventually, I had to stop. I needed purpose; God must have me here for some reason. I just needed to know what that was. I took to my Bible and immersed myself in the Word, hoping to find the answers I desperately needed. I, not surprisingly, found them. I found the answers I needed in Titus 2, in the call for the Titus 2 Mother in our current world state. It taught me that if I am focused on the LORD, on glorifying God, I won't fall prey or surrender myself or my social media pages to the devil. Instead, I will become a light to guide others to Him. We want the same for our daughters, for them to be a beacon, shining the light toward our heavenly Father with her good nature and edifying words and heart. Ephesians 4:29 says:

> *Let no corrupt communication proceed out of your mouth, but that which is good to the use of edifying, that it may minister grace unto the hearers.*

We can be grace-giving lights, God-spirited warriors who impart goodwill and wholesome teachings to others. We cannot fall prey. We cannot surrender. We must be warriors of God and teach our daughters to do the same, or they will be used by the devil. They, too, will hand over their tongues if we do not teach them otherwise. Holding one's tongue is hard. It's a challenge on the best of days, so we must be the change we wish to see in the world, the change we wish to see in God's kingdom and among our sisters. Our change can inspire and influence others. This change also validates our Titus 2 Motherhood and highlights the importance of self-control in a world lacking it. We must not disappear when the world is plunged into darkness. We must retain our composure and remind ourselves that there is more than one way to embody and exercise self-control...

Take Aways

- Lies and deceit are out there and aimed against us. They serve to trip us up. We must be aware of the truth and be in the Word so we can avoid being deceived.
- Watch your speech and remember its power to change hearts and character, affecting the very fruit you're trying to cultivate.
- Think about how you interact with your husband and if the language used toward each other is conducive to good fruit and adult behavior or if there are little ones repeating phrases or words.

Heart Probing Questions

1. Have you fallen for any of the feminist rhetoric? Why or why not?
2. Are your children aware of the war being waged against their gender? Why might you expose them to this battle and the importance of our Creator's perfect design?
3. Do you have a stance when it comes to abortion? Have you discussed it with your husband? Why or why not?

4. Do your children know about abortions? If not, when might you tell them?

5. Is the way you and your husband are communicating affecting your children?

CHAPTER 4

Sober Minded

P icture a drunk woman at a dinner party, slurring her words, falling about the place with an air of clumsiness that you didn't realize existed until you saw it yourself. Many of us have not only witnessed this kind of behavior, but we have also lived it, having had at least one such experience. In these experiences, judgment and self-control often go out the window. In Titus 2:3, Paul states that a Titus 2 Woman is 'not given too much wine.' While this is sound advice, we must go further to discover its deeper meaning: self-control and moderation. We are to resist excess in any area of daily life. We are not to be slaves to any substance, amusement, fashion, or attitude that doesn't please the LORD.

In the imagery gotten from the drunken woman, we can assume that those who are sober looking upon her might, through discernment or judgment, feel that she lacks self-control, moderation, and sense. In our society, moderation is rarely publicized and encouraged. It's quite the opposite. 'Take a load off,' 'Have a drink,' society tells us that we deserve to indulge ourselves and consume as much as our heart desires, as this will bring us much happiness. The truth is we must be careful of the desires of the flesh. As Christians, we are not to love the world but live within it (1 JHN 2:15.) Galatians 5:16-18 says:

> *This I say then, Walk in the Spirit, and ye shall not fulfil the lust of the flesh. For the flesh lusteth against the Spirit, and the Spirit against the flesh: and these are contrary the one to the other: so that ye cannot do the things that ye would. But if ye be led of the Spirit, ye are not under the law.*

Being in the word and spending time to connect with God will allow us to have a relationship with God and be better led by the spirit. When we give into fleshly wants, we cause a divide of allegiance that makes it hard for us to do what we are called or led to do.

TEMPTATIONS

The best show of self-control in the face of temptation and Earthly abundance is in Matthew 4:1-11:

Then was Jesus led up of the Spirit into the wilderness to be tempted of the devil. And when he had fasted forty days and forty nights, he was afterward an hungred. And when the tempter came to him, he said, If thou be the Son of God, command that these stones be made bread. But he answered and said, It is written, Man shall not live by bread alone, but by every word that proceedeth out of the mouth of God. Then the devil taketh him up into the holy city, and setteth him on a pinnacle of the temple, And saith unto him, If thou be the Son of God, cast thyself down: for it is written, He shall give his angels charge concerning thee: and in their hands they shall bear thee up, lest at any time thou dash thy foot against a stone. Jesus said unto him, It is written again, Thou shalt not tempt the Lord thy God. Again, the devil taketh him up into an exceeding high mountain, and sheweth him all the kingdoms of the world, and the glory of them; And saith unto him, All these things will I give thee, if thou wilt fall down and worship me. Then saith Jesus unto him, Get thee hence, Satan: for it is

*written, Thou shalt worship the Lord thy God, and
him only shalt thou serve. Then the devil leaveth
him, and, behold, angels came and ministered unto
him.*

For any average person without fear of the LORD,
the promise of simple riches and a prosperous life would be
enough for any devious character to gain allegiance.
However, for the Son of Man, allegiance is only for the
LORD our God. He is the only one worthy of loyalty, love,
and honor, being that He is good, righteous, and the
example of what love truly is. Satan offered Jesus all the
Earthly kingdoms in exchange for worship. In Jesus's
answer, he shows the standard to live by: we are to pledge
ourselves to the LORD alone and not falter in our promise
regardless of what offers might come. Truly, we have no
need for Earthly riches because God has given us the
greatest gift: the gift of grace. Ephesians 2:8-9 says:

*For by grace are ye saved through faith; and that
not of yourselves: it is the gift of God: Not of works,
lest any man should boast.*

Eternal life awaits those who have faith in Jesus.
That faith is our acceptance of His sacrifice. Our love and
gratitude for Jesus should influence us to stay faithful to
God. As Christians, we want to teach our children 'the way'
so that when faced with a society that goes against God,

they stand steadfast in faith and loyalty to the LORD. We must remember that our works are not what we do for salvation but what we do to please the LORD. Knowing that our works are like filthy rags when compared to the glory of God (ISA 64:6), we don't want our children to fall for the tricks and deceptions of the devil. We want them to know who their true adversary is and not hate those who fall prey to deception, for hatred doesn't change hearts. Love does. God asks us to love Him. Matthew 22:37-40 says:

> *Jesus said unto him, Thou shalt love the Lord thy God with all thy heart, and with all thy soul, and with all thy mind. This is the first and great commandment. And the second is like unto it, Thou shalt love thy neighbour as thyself. On these two commandments hang all the law and the prophets.*

Jesus tells us that the two greatest commandments are to love God and our neighbors as ourselves. And since we are made in His image, we should have love for ourselves because He made us and made us like Him (GEN 1:27).

Having too much can be tempting, especially when those sweet treats, drinks, and objects are associated with festivities, happiness, and the love of family and friends. We must be careful not to fall prey to the want for more and the pursuit of happiness. Happiness is fleeting and will leave us longing for something lasting. God's word has the solution for us. We can focus on the joy of Him, the joy of serving Him, knowing He loves us so much that He gave His only son so that we can live with Him forever (JHN 3:16.)

CONSUMERISM AND ITS FATHERS

It's no shocker that many people fall prey to indulgence and desire when happiness and consumerism are the main drivers within society. Instead of love, sacrifice and service, we have a shallow self-boosting. In times of crisis, leaders tell us to go out and buy stuff for the good of the economy. During these times, politicians could say anything, maybe something uplifting and action-provoking, something to get people enthusiastic about helping others and supporting each other through sharing resources, but no! 'Shop' and 'buy more stuff' are the directives given to the masses. Have a look at this quote from "The Father of Public Relations," Edward Bernays, in his 1928 book entitled *Propaganda*:

> *If we understand the mechanisms and motives of the group mind, it is now possible to control and regiment the masses according to our will without their knowing it. In almost every act of our daily lives, whether in the sphere of politics or business, in our social conduct or our ethical thinking, we are*

dominated by the relatively small number of persons who understand the mental processes and social patterns of the masses. It is they who pull the wires which control the public mind.

Here is another quote from Bernays' book *Propaganda*:

When I came back to the United States, I decided that if you could use propaganda for war, you could certainly use it for peace. And "propaganda" got to be a bad word because of the Germans using it, so what I did was to try and find some other words so we found the word "councelor of public relations."

PR is propaganda, just with a little more sophistication. Edward Bernays is the father of PR, but he was also Sigmund Freud's nephew; he took Freud's work and used it to form the basis of his teachings in PR. He wrote books such as "Crystallizing Public Opinion," "Propaganda," and "Public Relations," each of which outlines different techniques and tools to manipulate and sway the masses. These strategies are present in everyday politics, advertising, and television.

It's important to note that not all political, marketed, and televised rhetoric is malicious, deceptive, or evil on its own or in its entirety. Intention matters, and not everyone is out there to deceive. Some people genuinely want to make a positive change or create something helpful for the world. Still, we must address the problems we face, and though some people and companies may have pure intentions, plenty of others don't.

We are bombarded daily by countless advertisements that tell us we're not good enough, thin enough, bright enough, or clean enough, and the only way to be the best we can be is through the consumption of the products in front of our eyes. Let's look back at old advertisements, the language used to persuade consumption, and the issues these products caused within society. We get a good indication of what today's propaganda is doing to our children and us. Below is a slogan for 'L&M filter tip cigarettes':

Just What the Doctor Ordered!

An array of harmful products have always been advertised and put on the market. Health star ratings and government approval have been given to countless products, including those that were eventually deemed harmful. Examples I can think of just off the top of my head are asbestos, cigarettes, and sugar. We have seen many harmful products sweep through our society and devastate people's lives and health. Sugar is still debated, though its health impacts are more evident now than ever. Sugar is still added to countless products in the supermarket to the point where you'd be hard-pressed to find a product without sugar. Sugar consumption has been linked to diabetes and numerous other ailments due to its inflammatory-invoking properties. On May 10, 1971, issue of TIME, a pro-sugar ad appeared saying:

Sugar can be the willpower you need to undereat

Our children need our guidance in this arena because they, too, are being targeted. But how do we combat this? We can limit our exposure to advertisements through the following:

- Reduced social media and television consumption.
- Being in the Word and praying that our family does not fall prey to this issue and that we will be able to see through the lies being pushed toward us.
- De-cluttering and keeping our home free of unnecessary items.
- And finally, we can be conscientious in our purchases by not buying items without first having thought about them for some time and discussing them with our husbands.

We must make better choices now and set an example for our children to keep this fiasco of madness and consumerism out of our homes.

EATING HABITS

Using the mechanisms of PR, corporations, businesses, and governing bodies can push culturally pervasive narratives in order to sell their products and line their pockets. These advertisements are aimed not just at us but also at our children. We have ads that normalize unhealthy habits, encourage overconsumption, and glorify obesity. If we treat ourselves like a rubbish bin, eating any old garbage our eyes are drawn to, our bodies are significantly harmed, and our connection with our creator feels distant because we are no longer listening to Him but to our want for more. Food becomes an idol. This is not God's design for us. We are temples for the Holy Ghost, not a trash can.

I have fallen prey to this, as I find myself attached and stuck in seasons of unhealthy eating habits. I eat chocolate when I am on my period and also when I am feeling emotional turmoil; this shows an attachment to food I do not want to pass down. I have found myself searching for help in the pages of old-fashioned cookbooks like 'Mrs. Beeton's All About Cookery'. Women like her were celebrated as culinary masters of the home, but today, some of her ideas may seem a little unorthodox when turning to recipes involving sheep's heads and other strange animal parts that most people cut off and discard. In her time, most households were on the lookout for innovative ways to use scraps and off-cuts so nothing was left to waste. I confess I find myself wanting to cook with diligence and innovation as Beeton and other ladies of her time did. However, I can't say I find all of the ideas appetizing or encouraging. It can be easy to lack motivation when the reason to do something, such as cooking, isn't apparent or seems obsolete.

Food can bring us together; many say the kitchen is the heart of the home and when we boil down our daily family routines, mealtimes are the one needed constant that has us consistently slowing down to gather around a table. We have conversation and we break bread with one another. Breaking bread isn't just to sustain an innate need for sustenance, Luke 22:19 says:

> *And he took bread, and gave thanks, and brake it, and gave unto them, saying, This is my body which is given for you: this do in remembrance of me.*

Jesus tells us the significance of breaking bread by tying it to his sacrifice for us. He also showed us throughout his time among us, when he shared bread with thousands, Mark 6:41-43 says:

> *And when he had taken the five loaves and the two fishes, he looked up to heaven, and blessed, and brake the loaves, and gave **them** to his disciples to set before them; and the two fishes divided he among*

*them all. And they did all eat, and were filled. And
they took up twelve baskets full of the fragments,
and of the fishes.*

Food is a blessing from God; it's also a way to
forge bonds, cultivate lasting traditions, and show the love
of God. There is a reason why so many people say the
kitchen is the heart of the home.

My family and I fell for a movement and idolization
of veganism. We weren't just changing our diets. We were
'Vegan.' It became an obsession as we checked labels and
took our own food to family and friends' houses, thinking
we were avoiding putting pressure on them to make food
for us when, in reality, we were offending them. It was a
strange time and a time when I became incredibly skinny
and sickly, to the point where my mother asked us to stop.
But we couldn't. We had become part of the cult-like group
and made our way into friendships and social media groups
that aligned with nothing else: idolization of food,
regimented and cult-like. If someone said anything remotely
against veganism, they were attacked and treated as an
outcast within the circles we had become a part of. We were
modeling this for our child; he was eating as we did, and
seeing how we acted as we refused to eat certain things, he
spoke of others who chose to eat differently in unnecessary
and ungodly ways. It was sad, and now, since reading 1
Timothy 4:1-6, I see why:

Now the Spirit speaketh expressly, that in the latter times some shall depart from the faith, giving heed to seducing spirits, and doctrines of devils; Speaking lies in hypocrisy; having their conscience seared with a hot iron; **Forbidding to marry, and commanding to abstain from meats, which God hath created to be received with thanksgiving of them which believe and know the truth.** *For every creature of God is good, and nothing to be refused, if it be received with thanksgiving: For it is sanctified by the word of God and prayer. If thou put the brethren in remembrance of these things, thou shalt be a good minister of Jesus Christ, nourished up in the words of faith and of good doctrine, whereunto thou hast attained.*

This moment in time was prophesized, the push for veganism, the devil's game to harm God, His creation, and create a new idol to worship in consumption. It's important to note here that I am not saying everyone who is vegan is involved in idol worship, as I have seen some people partake in the diet without a dogmatic approach, but this is rare. Many people are taking the consumption of meat offensively, calling it harmful to our planet and an act of evil on animals. Animal rights activists and people who identify as vegan take a firm stance that everyone should be on a plant-based diet, but this is a doctrine of man. Paul said, "For every creature of God *is* good, and nothing to be refused, if it be received with thanksgiving" in 1 Timothy 4:4. There is nothing wrong with us eating meat. That being said, I do believe there are good and bad ways to treat animals, and we humans have been given the task of subduing and taking care of the Earth and its animal inhabitants, and this should be done in love.

A DRUNKEN FATHER

I grew up with a father who believed having a drink was a reasonable way to end the day, that a hard day's work warranted a beer or glass of wine, but one would regularly turn into many more. Our recycling bin was often full of empty bottles before the end of the week, leaving no room for the normal cereal boxes or food packets most people have. His drinking, on occasion, would peter out, but only after a massive blow-out that left smashed or broken belongings, doors off hinges, and family or friends alienated after a punch-up. The apologies would come after and were often followed by a decrease in alcohol consumption. The tension would build every cycle until the next time he lost it. Boy, did he lose it! When he was raging, it was like he was gone, and the devil had replaced him. His eyes glazed over, and his demeanor seemed menacing and hateful. At the best of times, he was awful, hurtful, and manipulative, but there was something especially evil about him when he lost all control in his fits of rage. As a child, I can tell you it was horrific, and I remember hiding under my covers many times, holding my breath, almost praying he didn't come up the stairs for us. There were times when my sisters and I were together, huddled, cuddling, and crying over the events unfolding downstairs. Sometimes it was easy to hear, while other times shouting and screaming blended to form one big thunderous noise that seemed to go on forever, until the moment that was dreaded most of all, the silence, the sign it might be over, but also the sign someone was on the move. The fear would amp us up, and I distinctly remember holding my breath as I heard footsteps toward the bedroom. Thankfully, it was always mom coming in to check on us and try to make us feel better. But I never felt better about him, nor did I feel protected by her because I knew he was physically capable of going through her and that one day he might.

In my teen years, my feelings of anger, fear, and resentment melded into one foolish teenage girl who would speak out of turn and build the anger in her father like a sport. I remember not even thinking about what I was doing and only thinking about how angry I was at him. I didn't care about anything or anyone else. I was trying to fill the emptiness I felt. I didn't think of my mother and how she would have the task of calming him back down to prevent getting another smashed plate, broken door, or nose. Mum would command me to leave the room when he erupted. She would then spend the rest of the afternoon and night calming him and talking him round to a normal state; this wasn't always possible and did, at times, lead to an angry tirade through the house.

I doubt my mother was surprised to see me acting in such ways toward my father; after all, I had always been the one to say, "No, I don't forgive you" when my father asked for forgiveness after one of many drunken rampages. Everyone else would say, "It's okay, daddy. I forgive you." Not me. I stood firm in what my mother had taught me: if you keep doing something you say sorry for, sorry doesn't mean anything. Even at the age of five, I told my father point blank, "I do not forgive you, and I am not speaking to you." I held my silence toward him for three months. It was either stubbornness or determination, and it was effective in building even more animosity between my father and me. He had already been treating me with less care than my sisters.

In the end, I removed myself. I could see I was making life harder for my mother and sister and that life was harder for me with him as an influence. I moved out as soon as possible and moved in with my now-husband. My husband rarely drinks; he usually reserves drinking for every now and again. I was glad he was not a drinker as my experience with my father taught me to hate alcohol, but as if in jest on the occasions my husband has drunk a little too much, he is actually lovely to the point of being more affectionate towards me. The juxtaposition is almost comical from one dominant man in my life to the next. The resulting thought is that the alcohol wasn't the problem, but rather, the man who lacked control was.

I look back on childhood now as a great tool. I use my un-godly experiences to strengthen my faith and live a more God-centred life. Self-control is not an easy trait to master, but Galatians 5:22-25 says:

> *But the fruit of the Spirit is love, joy, peace, longsuffering, gentleness, goodness, faith, Meekness, temperance: against such there is no law. And they that are Christ's have crucified the flesh with the affections and lusts. If we live in the Spirit, let us also walk in the Spirit.*

We as believers don't have to rely on our own strength of will; we have the Holy Spirit within us. By walking in the Spirit, we become more like Christ. We want this for our children—for them to bear fruit and to know God. When we walk in the Spirit, we feel more connected to our Creator, and we become visible examples of faith for our children to follow.

GROWING REALISATION

We are all aware of the possible and often inevitable effects of substance abuse, whether it be alcohol or something else. It's imperative to note that the Bible never forbids us from drinking wine; however, we must use our discernment, consider others' consciences, and uphold our testimony to the world to guide our actions. The life of a believer is not necessarily one of prosperity, and it certainly is not one of indulgence. If we exemplify drunkenness for our children, we undermine our God-given position and authority to lead and guide them in a faithful life.

We are told temperance or self-control requires consistency, so we must be cautious of intemperance. All we do is to be tempered by the glory of God. 1 Corinthians 10:31 says:

> *Whether therefore ye eat, or drink, or whatsoever ye do, do all to the glory of God.*

In this, we are safeguarded from seeking glory for ourselves, from becoming prideful and self-righteous. In God, we can trust; He will lead us to do good works. As Titus 2 Mothers, we can guide our daughters as God intends, by not only looking to His Word but also listening to the Holy Spirit. Having self-control not only nurtures our discipline as followers of God but also our teachable hearts, which our children can perceive through our good actions. Jesus said in Matthew 5:16:

> *Let your light so shine before men, that they may see your good works, and glorify your Father which is in heaven.*

This self-control and discipline can be shown and practiced with more than just food and drink. Upon the arrival of our first son, my husband was very much an avid gamer. He loved looking at trailers and reviews, playing the games themselves, or watching others play. It was a constant thing in his life that had started in early childhood. He clung to it. What he felt was a need to play. Our son, of course, was significantly affected; he became addicted as he learned to play the games for himself. At the time we had not found Christ, and the world was approving of our parenting methods and letting our three-year-old play on the Switch that had been designed for a child as young as him to be able to play. He got good fast, and I was horrified that he had learned to play games but could not communicate well with language, which shouldn't have come as a surprise given that all his attention was on playing games and not on learning how to speak. I eventually told my husband I felt something was wrong and that our son needed to stop playing games. This was the start of my husband's journey away from games, too, not that he fully knew it. He had, on occasion, said he would stop playing or that it was a waste of time, but he kept playing and refusing to give up what he felt was part of him and his history. It wasn't until my husband saw the difference no screens were making to our son that he realized his habit was holding him back. My son's ability to communicate, focus, and learn significantly increased.

My husband found that all his spare time was, at the time, spent on gaming, so he was always saying he didn't have time to do anything. After a lot of back and forth to and from games, buying, selling, and repurchasing them, my husband eventually settled for a less dogmatic approach, removing the 'all or nothing' idea, and now rarely plays games. He instead has seasons where he might play a little more or less and seasons where he doesn't play at all. He now has more time to work on what he is passionate about, which God has given him a heart for.

Being a person of faith makes it somewhat easier to have self-control because there is a true and loving reason for it beyond the physically obvious. It's sad that so many people slip down the devil's pit and never take the long journey that the lifeline (Jesus Christ) provides us, up and out of the hole. We must be the example of this lifeline-taking journey, clinging to our Savior, Jesus, and embracing love, integrity, and self-control. Our works and discipline speak volumes of the LORD and will shine a light upon Him, guiding His sons and daughters to Him. We must be honest about our faults and shortcomings, even telling our children that we wish to break habits we possess and how they will hopefully find this embodiment of self-control much easier than we have. We can explain to them that the Holy Spirit will help them as they grow and learn, just as it is helping us. Telling them allows God to work His wonders and show our children His glory through our changing hearts. When we witness miracles, it is hard to be out of aith or deny our Creator. This is our opportunity, and thank God we have been given it. We can use these moments of change to inspire and teach goodness...

TAKE AWAYS

- We must exercise self-control in all things.
- Self-control is about more than just food and drink. It's about a life practice of not overindulging oneself in anything.
- Focusing on bringing glory to God in all things helps us to grow in faith and shines a light to God, growing His kingdom.
- Your self-control can be part of your testimony

HEART PROBING QUESTIONS

1. Is there an area in your life or home where you lack self-control? Why? How might you help yourself rectify this? Is it obvious to your children? How might you talk to them about it and glorify God in your journey away from the habit?

2. Have you known anyone who seems to lack self-control? What kind of person were they? Did they show fruit?

3. Do you see any self-control issues with your children? Why or why not? Are they in need of something? Is it necessary to remove anything from the home?

CHAPTER 5

Integrity of a Titus 2 Woman

In Titus 2:3, Paul writes that Titus 2 Women are to be "teachers of good things," to live with spiritual integrity, or in other words, practice what we preach. I'm sure by now, at some point, you have been called a hypocrite, or at the very least, you've seen one in action. As mothers, we can be sure that from time to time, we may say we will do something with good intentions but lack time to do it. Yet we teach our children that 'words have meaning' and 'if we say we will do something, we should do it'. Trying to live up to godly teachings is tough, and it takes time, work, and a willingness or teachable heart to change. We are not born knowing how to be the perfect, godly woman or mother; we learn, grow, and then become. We must also be realistic, knowing that perfection is humanly impossible. Instead, we must aim for our ideal selves. Hopefully, we become these Amazing-Titus-2-Godly-Women, whose walk speaks louder than their words, as actions often do. We are to place our daily lives in God's control. We are not to overindulge ourselves; we are not to be overweight gluttons; we are not to be pleasure-hungry; we are not to be malicious talkers. We are to have integrity in our lives, practicing what we preach and teaching through the practice of doing.

OVERINDULGE OURSELVES

With the high-tech propaganda of today, as discussed in the previous chapter, it takes a lot of work to get away from the 'shout' to consume and buy 'stuff'. Imagine going to the shop with your daughter, and you go through the shopping aisle specifically for girls; beautiful things are everywhere: Dolls wearing the latest fashion trends, pretend make-up, pretty dresses, you name it. Those with Daughters big enough to skip through a shopping aisle may already hear 'Can I have that, Mummy?'

As Mothers, we are influenced by advertisers to believe we need a series of products in order to confirm our feminine identity. We see Ads showing a variety of women often smiling or looking successful wearing Designer Shoes, Make-Up, and the latest fashion trends. Sound familiar? From childhood to womanhood, we are hit with the same messaging; to be a woman we need to look a certain way for the betterment of ourselves, our families, society, or anything else that we may place value on. The women who fall head over heels for these deceptions become women who are of the world. 1 John 2:15-16 says:

> *Love not the world, neither the things that are in the world. If any man love the world, the love of the Father is not in him. For all that is in the world, the lust of flesh, and the lust of the eyes, and the pride of life, is not of the Father, but of the world.*

John speaks of not loving the world, as loving the world is not of the Father. When we focus on our love for the LORD, we can better walk in the Spirit. The fruit of the Spirit enables us to resist temptation. Rooting ourselves in the word and His sacrifice will help us focus on the eternal. That, I am sure, is something we all want for our children. So, how can we approach our daughter when she asks, 'Can I have that, Mummy?' We can tell her the truth: corporations and industries use the bright colors and shiny boxes to make us want things that we don't need and that won't give us lasting joy. You can also describe how these products are made; someone, perhaps even a child, paid very little or not at all, reduced to a life of modern slavery made this or part of this. There are many conversations we can have with our children concerning slavery and the exploitation of people presently and in history. The truth helps us take the rose-tinted glasses off and see the countless products around us for what they are: desires of the flesh and a distraction.

OVER-WEIGHTED GLUTTONS

This title could be triggering for some, as in Western societies, it is politically correct to promote that being overweight is healthy and beautiful, despite a clear disregard and purposeful blindness toward any factual literature relevant to the subject. Instead of entertaining the idea that something might be wrong, we must affirm that everything is okay, and we should be happy to maintain any size our body can supposedly fit into. God's Word contradicts this notion, implying that we should have stewardship over our bodies. 1 Corinthians 3:16-17 says:

> *Know ye not that ye are the temple of God, and that the Spirit of God dwelleth in you? If any man defile the temple of God, him shall God destroy; for the temple of God is holy which temple ye are.*

Our bodies are a temple for the LORD. We, as believers, know we are not our own. We were bought at a high price. Jesus died for us. We have dominion over our bodies, and we must be careful with what we put in and on them, for these things provide the body with its nutrients and affect its functioning. If we do not look after our bodies, we are not loving the LORD as He commanded. We cannot be overweight and healthy; it's an oxymoron. This any-size-body-is-beautiful mentality has filtered down into the schooling system and now corrupts the next generation of thought. Being overweight is no longer a sign of improper nutrition and a sedentary lifestyle but is considered inspirational and courageous. These inspirational women dress half-naked and are featured 'bravely' in many articles, photoshoots, and video campaigns to try to normalize this over-indulgent lifestyle. I am not saying that someone's worth is solely based on their outer appearance, merely that we should see things as they are and recognize that being overweight shows a lack of self-control. This comes from a place of love; it is not loving to lie to yourself or others, no matter how much the truth hurts.

We see a lot of influencers online telling us the best ways to be healthy, and it looks like they have it down pat. They appear as if they never falter, but they're human just like you and me, and they too have off days. Honesty, understanding, and love are the ways we can combat unrealistic expectations and politically correct rhetoric that form untrue narratives. My husband has recently spoken with me about his weight and how his enjoyment of food has caused him to over-indulge even when he is no longer hungry. His solution to this is to limit his portion sizes and/or fast. He and I have always been fairly skinny. His was more so due to his active lifestyle and mine was due to a lack of nutrition. I ate very small portions and rarely indulged in sweet treats. I can recall countless occasions as a child where I didn't want to finish my dinner, and the reward of dessert did little to entice my appetite. Since having children, this has changed somewhat. I have a healthy appetite, most likely due to breastfeeding, and I have gone back to a steady weight after having each baby. However, being faced with grief, which I will talk about more in a later chapter, and having my fourth child has put me in a state of unhealthy habits. I've never been that active, but now my age demands me to start or face the consequences of inaction such as aches, pains, body fat, and decay.

My experience with weight has taught me that being skinny doesn't necessarily mean being healthy, and there can be seasons where we falter from healthy habits due to grief, fatigue, or pain entering our lives. The important thing to do here is to continue getting back onto the healthy habit bandwagon and keep reintroducing those good habits into your daily routine.

We can teach our children this self-control by not having dessert every night or treats every day and by eating until we are full. We can explain this to our children and teach them that they don't have to eat everything on their plate if they are full. Many parents get confused with this sentiment, saying, 'But how will I ever get them to eat their vegetables?' The answer is simple: remind them that they 'will get nothing else until the next mealtime.' If this is a regular occurrence and you feel the need to do something drastic, you could save what they don't eat for the next meal. Be strong in your choices, knowing that eventually, hunger is stronger than the will not to eat a vegetable. Have faith and pray for your child to have a teachable heart and to eat what they require. If you or your partner are struggling with unhealthy habits, pray for them and yourself; you can also ask them to pray for you.

PLEASURE HUNGRY

This is a societal driving force, an idea sold to us that life is meant to be pleasurable and enjoyable at every turn. We are told there's no need to suffer, and all we have to do is buy this or have that or eat that to be happy. These things we know are lies. It's frustrating, but we can see that positive reinforcement and praise work well to motivate our children. Propaganda has twisted this principle into something ugly: 'You want to be of the world to be happy.' Happiness, a fleeting emotion, is represented as a career goal and destination. Deepak Chopra said:

Happiness is the ultimate goal. It is the goal of all other goals.

You cannot be 'happy-ful,' but you can be joyful because we do more than feel joy. We embody it. Joy is in the heart and of the soul, while happiness is on the face and of the moment. Galatians 5:22-23 says:

But the fruit of the Spirit is love, joy, peace, longsuffering, gentleness, goodness, faith, Meekness, temperance: against such there is no law.

Joy is not fleeting. We feel it, and we can uplift others with it. It's a building experience, but happiness is short-lived and doesn't provide the lasting fulfillment that joy does. Joy is transcendent, something we can experience even in tough times and bring to even the hardest of situations, but happiness is reactive, something we feel, usually when things are going well for us. So, society preaches that we aim to achieve a fleeting feeling as a goal for life. If you're unhappy, you're encouraged to drop what you are doing and re-evaluate, redirecting to a totally new reality, dropping everything that isn't 'happiness-invoking.'

Our intentions become shallow, caught up in details that don't truly matter. Isaiah 61:10 says:

> *I will greatly rejoice in the LORD, my soul shall be joyful in my God; for he hath clothed me with the garments of salvation, he hath covered me with the robe of righteousness, as a bridegroom decketh himself with ornaments, and as a bride adorneth herself with her jewels.*

Here Isaiah speaks of being clothed in salvation and wearing a robe of righteousness as gifts from God. This time of rejoicing is coupled with that of a wedding day when a bride and groom come together in matrimony to become one flesh for life. We as believers have been gifted salvation and righteousness by faith forever. Our relationship with God is now eternal and that is cause for celebration.

God's word tells us to delight ourselves in the LORD (PSA 37:4) and to rejoice when God corrects us as he is the one whose 'hands make whole' (JOB 5:17-27). That which pleases the LORD is good (PSA 5:4). We want our children to do what the LORD wills them to do. We want them to obey God and us so they can be led out of temptations and not fall prey to the world's glamour and flashing lights. We can only do this if we are also in our right mind, not falling prey to the happiness lies and traps.

We must embody joy by being in the word and spending those precious free moments praying to strengthen our connection to the LORD.

MALICIOUS TALKER

I have described this in length in previous chapters, but it's always good to reinforce the importance of not allowing the devil to use your tongue for evil. We must embed Ephesians 4:29 within our minds, which says:

> *Let no corrupt communications proceed out of your mouth, but that which is good to use of edifying, that it may minister grace unto the hearers.*

The saying "think before you speak" comes to mind when I read this verse because that was a teaching most of us were raised with. Communicating is so easy now, though; we can write something and send it. With predictive text and now the addition of things like AI, God only knows where the art of conversation is headed. This is why we have to consciously speak wisely. We should be slow to speak, considering what is good and edifying. Our example of speaking rightly, with the intention to do good and build someone up in strength and faith, will impact and shape our children's tongues. We have the chance to make gossip, harsh, and bitter words foreign to them. The best way to control our own tongues is to filter what we hear. If we regularly listen to people gossiping and swearing in podcasts and talk shows, it should be of no surprise that we begin to copy. Of course, being in the world may, on occasion, cause us to slip up, but we should aim to minimize ungodly input for a better output. Regularly reading the Word and prayer can keep us mindful and walking in the Spirit. Consistency is key, so no matter how many times we might fail—and we will, sometimes in great detrimental ways, FAIL, we continue and trust that the LORD will guide us, soften our hearts, and lead us away from temptation.

Although we are not saved through works, our works can shine a light on God. Our works can be a testimony of faith and a glorification of God. Our works are how God helps soften hearts and bring His sons and daughters willingly to Him. We shine the light that leads to God. That same light also illuminates His creation all around us, exposing His obvious work and goodness. With so many distractions, it's hard for people to come to the Father without a real fight on their hands. For our daughters to be strong in faith, we must model this for them, this persistence, this determination to grow, have a teachable heart, and be active in good works so they might copy and do the same. 1 Thessalonians 5:5-11 says:

> *Ye are all the children of light, and the children of the day: we are not of the night, nor of darkness.*

*Therefore let us not sleep, as **do** others; but let us watch and be sober. For they that sleep sleep in the night; and they that be drunken are drunken in the night. But let us, who are of the day, be sober, putting on the breastplate of faith and love; and for an helmet, the hope of salvation. For God hath not appointed us to wrath, but to obtain salvation by our Lord Jesus Christ, Who died for us, that, whether we wake or sleep, we should live together with him. Wherefore comfort yourselves together, and edify one another, even as also ye do.*

Our integrity as Titus 2 Mothers shines brightly and encourages not only our daughters and husbands but also other mothers to do the same. We can then become the Titus 2 Woman, a woman of influence and inspiration to younger and, in some cases, older women who may have lacked the teaching themselves. We, mothers, must take on this burden of building up motherhood, womanhood, and wifehood, for it is being demolished. We must be the warriors left standing on the mount of rubble, faithfully clasping our hands together, looking up to the LORD in prayer. We must become God's faithful servants and be role models for the younger women around us…

TAKE AWAYS

- We must practice what we preach so we are not labeled hypocrites.
- Integrity is something we should maintain in all facets of life, including what we buy, eat, wear, and do.
- The Bible doesn't preach a life of happiness but rather a joy found in faith and obedience to the LORD, regardless of the season.
- We can make evil seem foreign to our children by speaking only those things which are edifying.
- Our integrity has the power to rebuild motherhood, wifehood, and womanhood from the rubble to which it has been reduced within the current societal climate.

HEART PROBING QUESTIONS

1. Have you been called a hypocrite?
2. Do you overconsume?
3. Do you fall into the happiness trap and set goals to achieve it?
4. How can you make changes in yourself today that will impact your family home?

5. Do you speak words that are edifying?

6. Do you ever fall prey to the devil and speak maliciously?

CHAPTER 6

Role Model and Influence

I want you to imagine yourself before having children. I
know at this point it's probably hard to do, but we can think
on it. Before having children, we thought we knew what
parenting was, what motherhood entailed, and what it
would feel like. Only reality was different and a lot less
rose-tinted. All those things we said we wouldn't do or say
torture us as we hear our mother's or father's words slip
from our lips. It's like a bad dream except there's no waking
up to a soft pillow beneath your head. Your wake-up-reality-
call is a screaming child in the middle of Kmart or a
seemingly endless bout of crying after telling your child the

word no; can we even use that word? Still, we change, grow, and realize many of our beliefs about parenting and motherhood were probably wrong. Our disdain or upset over our parents' methods will somewhat diminish over time, and we may discover a more understanding, less self-righteous, less bitter version of ourselves. Many of our parents' choices are exposed for what they were: what they thought was best to do. Because most of us, hopefully, are doing our best, surely no one comes into something such as parenting to fail on purpose. No! We want to strive to do well. But as we are sinful and gullible in many respects, we become something we never expected, a hypocrite to our younger selves. Matthew 7:5 says:

> *Thou hypocrite, first cast out the beam out of thine own eye; and then shalt thou see clearly to cast out the mote out of thy brother's eye.*

The important thing here is not to judge but instead focus on servitude to our own families so we can better ourselves, using discernment regarding our parents' shortfalls so we might learn from their mistakes and do better in our own homes. It is important to remember that we will inevitably make our own mistakes. We must remember our inclination to sin, just like every other human being, before trying to tell anyone else how they are doing things wrong. We can save judgment for God. Instead, we must share the knowledge we learn through practice, research, and discernment.

When Paul writes about this Titus 2 Woman, he is referring to a woman who is past raising her children. This may be because, as mothers presently raising children, we are learning as we go and working through our own hang-ups, sinning against our children and ourselves at the same time. We learn and become so much more through teaching, cultivating, and leading our children that a certain level of wisdom and understanding is accomplished. We have the opportunity, as mothers, to acknowledge our role within our daughters' lives. The Titus 2 woman is required in the community to help younger women. Our daughters are young women in need of our guidance; let us take becoming this Titus 2 mother seriously so we can grow the godly qualities of a Titus 2 woman.

TITUS 2 WOMAN ROLE MODEL

If you wish to further your journey to becoming a Titus 2 Woman, look to older women who could be considered Titus 2 Women, having faithfully raised their children. Read books on the subject of Christian living on motherhood and mothering wisdom. Our learning should be a mixture of face-to-face interactions, through the church or gatherings, and books, such as Christian living books and blogs. We should approach this as we would the Bible. We don't just read the word. We go to church, listen to pastors, and sometimes, we meet or talk with missionaries and fellow believers, hearing testimonies that strengthen faith. Likewise, we must strengthen our motherhood and our faithful child-rearing. Some of us are in a long or difficult season where we have been unable to attend church or congregate with fellow believers. There are plenty of online resources now for us to still grow in faith and build ourselves in spiritual maturation. There are courses, sermons, and books such as this one that delve into people's lives and experiences. However, it is important to use discernment on this journey before consuming anything that claims to be rooted in Christianity. While this is a discussion that could fill a whole book, there are two areas that are important to be aware of, and we can think of them as two sides of the same coin. One side teaches a prosperity gospel where through works we can earn blessings from God and have whatever we want, and the other side teaches that to make it to heaven we must focus on the teacher's subjective standard of works, making us dependent on a Man for salvation. Here we can see the similarities of both doctrines effectively putting the believer into bondage of the discernment of the "teacher". They do this through the use of vague language and often by taking difficult and obscure passages out of context to fit their own purposes and beliefs.

It's important to not be fearful of the truth and to trust God with this matter. I would encourage you to seek advice from your partner in the Lord and to be completely honest in your journey, bringing your issues to God not in fear but humbling yourself. 1 Corinthians 8:2 says:

> *And if any man think that he knoweth any thing, he knoweth nothing yet as he ought to know.*

Here, Paul is telling us to be diligent, to seek wisdom and not be prideful thinking we know anything.

Also, be wary of those who claim to have the keys to the kingdom. Salvation is not for sale; it is a free gift. The works taught in this book are meant to be edifying, but we are to do all these things out of love for God, not the fear of damnation. John 11:25-26 says:

> *Jesus said unto her, I am the resurrection, and the life: he that believeth in me, though he were dead, yet shall he live: And whosoever liveth and believeth in me shall never die. Believest thou this?*

Faith is our salvation.

When looking for a Titus 2 Woman to role model, keep the following in mind: Titus 2:4 says, "That they may teach the younger women." The word 'teach' is admonish in the NKJV, train in NIV, and encourage in the NAS; the context and words explain this older woman's actions, words, and guidance to teach, explain, encourage, train, and hold young women accountable to a standard unfamiliar yet vital to their success in marriage and family life. According to Paul in Titus 2, the older-in-the-faith-godly-woman of the church is to…

- Behave like a holy priestess of the almighty God,
- Show restraint and discipline of appetite and words,
- Live what she speaks so that the younger women want to learn from her how to live a life pleasing to the LORD,
- Love her husband and children,
- Be discreet,
- Be chaste/pure,
- Be a keeper of the home and
- Be obedient to her husband.

We have an almost impossible job these days if you come from a faithless household or went through normal public education. Then we also have the seemingly endless onslaught of anti-Christian and ungodly rhetoric.

GOD-GIVEN ROLES AND GENDER DYSPHORIA

You would have seen the desecration of our God-given roles as men and women and the very genders themselves. Genesis 1:27 says:

So God created man in his own image, in the image of God created he him; male and female created he them.

The LGBTQ movement seems to have gained enough traction to infiltrate every facet of our society, including education, the law, and churches. The sentiments of the movement identified in the Bible as sin are being paraded as beautiful and by design. There are two genders: male and female. To say otherwise implies there is a problem in society that needs remedying through voluntary counsel and support. Of course, there is the occasional odd case where a person is born with both male and female parts, but this is rare and therefore, literally by definition, far from normal. There seems to be a push for teachings on gender dysphoria to muddy the waters of the God-given genders and create a choice where, genetically and physically, there isn't one. We must use our words for truth, telling our children repetitively (or whenever we can) what gender they are. We must solidify their sense of being and place so that no amount of confusion or trickery will enter. I remember feeling swayed in school, questioning whether I was quote 'Bi' (as in liking boys and girls). Of course, I found I liked boys, more specifically, my husband, and I still like him a lot – thank God. I think it's important to mention here that we all sin and fall short of God.

We must always look to Jesus in the way that we treat others. Jesus spent most of his time here with sinners, loving, teaching, and guiding them. Hateful and harsh treatment of those who sin will not remove sin nor help those caught in sin. There is no need for malice or mistreatment of these people. They are sinners, just like we are. Saying that, I don't believe we should invite these LGBTQ sentiments into the church, but we should welcome those who come knocking earnestly and humbly and, with God's grace, pray that they may establish a faithful heart. This is where our words can become edifying and uplifting to those who need them most.

AN EXPERIENCE IN EDUCATION

As we discuss role models and influence, we can only move forward once we have covered the topic of schooling. We must think long and hard about the influences and role models we want in our children's lives before making a final decision about education. Teachers and peers become the main influence in our children's lives when they attend public or private school. Unless you know every kid, every parent, and every teacher, you really have no idea of the influences forced upon your child. Even knowing these people can be a blinding experience as we still don't know what they do behind closed doors. Please don't be blinded. Some of you may be reading and thinking, 'Well, my child goes to a Christian school.' To that, I ask the same questions as any other parent sending their child to school: do you know the people there? Do you know the curriculum back to front? If you don't know these things, how can you be sure that the influences before your child are good? Of course, not everyone has the ability to homeschool or to spend the time getting involved with their children's school. If this is the case for you, do what you can to converse with your child in the car and on camping trips or holidays. Although your child's biggest influences will be at school, you can still impart lessons, wisdom, understanding, and model all the fruits you wish to see in them. It's also a good idea to give them a little insight into your own struggles and failings, not putting up a façade of perfection. In this way, when they inevitably struggle in their own journey even as adults, they can be honest with themselves and take responsibility to make changes for the better.

I can't say I had the typical high school experience, and I won't pretend that my experience didn't impact my choice to homeschool my children. You see, my mother worked at my school, and the teachers got to know her. They all got chummy and began to hang out outside of school hours, mainly at the local pub twice a week. That may sound fine and normal, except the location of their meeting eventually evolved or rather devolved, as things do, into karaoke nights at my house once a week. It was a strange way to enter high school for a young girl just entering her teens. I knew my teachers on a personal level. Occasionally, I had the unfortunate experience of finding my history or drama teachers on the sofa or games room floor hung over after a spring break-worthy night. At first, I was unsure of how these things affected me. As an adult looking back, it's easier to distinguish and understand the actions of these teachers as a need for friendship, love, and connection. However, as a parent, this makes me all the more aware of the fact that people in positions of authority are not always what they might appear to be despite their position and title. This is not necessarily a bad thing, but it's useful to know in order to make the best choices.

QUALIFICATION

The culture of today promotes the idea that it's okay to hand our children over for someone else to teach, telling us 'We are underqualified to teach our own children and 'it's a position best left to the professionals who have trained and spent time studying it.' However, it's important to note that if we are underqualified, it is because of the education we received. The same system that 'failed' us is the system we are told is better for our children than our own methods. I am a homeschooling Mama and a passionate advocate for it. Upon research and watching my own children grow, I've found homeschooling breeds creativity and, most importantly, a love of learning. The biggest issue with modern schooling is how it can suck the enjoyment out of learning and only aims to prepare you for a life working for someone else. You don't leave school knowing how to do your taxes, how to run a business, or how to make your talents, skills, and ideas useful and profitable in the world.

I started homeschooling my eldest son before I was Christian. I had noticed political arguments about race, gender, climate change, and so much more entering into the classroom, not in a way to build a child's knowledge, but to indoctrinate them into politically fueled arguments and narratives, such as 'White people are privileged.' This is taught without considering the countless white people who have nowhere to live and nothing to eat. 'Racism is when a white person judges and mistreats someone who is black.' This then leads young people to think that any racism toward white people is reverse racism and doesn't exist, even though racism is about anyone who judges someone else based on their color or ethnicity. I could go on, but I digress. I didn't want my child pumped full of these ideologies and teachings. I admit the first few years of homeschooling were tough, and I had no idea what to do or how to do it. I searched for answers in books, blogs, and YouTube videos, hoping to find the secret to success.

After becoming a Christian, what I would teach and, more importantly, how I would teach became clear. A big focus for us is missionaries, saints, and the world around us. We look at the history of humanity through missionaries first and bring in all the other information through old encyclopedias and occasional online resources and videos. My eldest does research projects, and this year he is writing a novel at the age of eight. So much more can be accomplished by our children when they have the time and space to learn, enjoy, and experiment. For that reason, our lessons aren't rigidly set. We will delve into a topic and go as far as desired before moving on to the next topic, even if that exploration and investigation lasts a month. The most fruitful studies have come from missionary stories and looking at how different people live around the world. We have great conversations about the differences and similarities between people and living, as well as the beauty of diversity in the world. We bring God into every school day. This is not something I set as a must but rather something that has happened. My children want to hear the word; they want to perform enactments and know more about the stories from 'the Bible times,' as we say.

It can take time to get confident in homeschooling, like four years, at least that's how it was for me. I have found much comfort in reminding myself that God has blessed me with these children for a reason and charged me with their upbringing. God has made me their guide and authority while they're young. So, I cannot hand this role over to someone else and think that fruit will grow if I don't spend my time cultivating them…

Take Aways

- We must be aware of the enemies' attacks and narratives.
- We need to be well-versed in our God-given roles so we can teach them to our children.
- Schooling is something every parent must discuss to be sure they're doing the right thing for their family.

Heart Probing Questions

1. Does your child know what gender they are?
2. Is there a way you can better solidify your child's gender and role?
3. How is your child or children schooled right now? How is this schooling affecting them?
4. If you don't homeschool, is it a possibility for your family? Could it be a better fit for your family than public school?
5. What influences are in your child's life currently? How are these influences affecting your child?

PART 2
Three Years Later…

CHAPTER 7

Love Your Husband

I want you to imagine your son getting married and your daughter-in-law (his wife) treating him as you treat your husband. Will you be happy, worried, or concerned? I bet most of us would feel one of the latter emotions. Our children absorb our teachings and may find themselves with a partner who mirrors our actions. Therefore, we must understand and be mindful of the examples we set. There was a time in the New Testament, after Christ, when Paul found a significant problem in young marriages; these marriages were filled with lovelessness and disdain. In response to this problem, Paul proposed deploying older-in-the-faith women (Titus 2 Women) to train the younger women; to become their husband's dearest and most intimate friend and partner. The sentiment was that women were not born knowing how to be loving, caring, romantic wives, but that they could learn those skills through mentorship.

DOWNPLAYING THE MARITAL RELATIONSHIP

Today's married women are often told that if they're unhappy in marriage, they can "just get a divorce," with phrases like "It shouldn't be this hard" and "There's plenty more fish in the sea." However, a fruitful and long-lasting relationship requires commitment, work, time, love, and cultivation to maintain. It's clear that society views marriage as a test for a relationship, and if it "doesn't work out," a couple can simply get a divorce, but Genesis 2:24 says:

> *Therefore shall a man leave his father and his mother, and shall cleave unto his wife: and they shall be one flesh.*

Here we see marriage is not an afterthought or a trial run. Marriage is a sanctified relationship. It is where a man and a woman go from being two individuals to becoming one. Our husbands need an emotionally and physically satisfying relationship just as we do. When these needs are met, we help safeguard their hearts and minds (1 COR 7:1-9.) from attraction and distraction in the wicked world around them. Proverbs 18:22 says:

> *Whoso findeth a wife findeth a good thing, and obtaineth favour of the LORD.*

Marriage is a good thing, a blessing. We don't have to face the world alone. We have someone to share our burdens and life with.

CHOOSE LOVE

If we are honest with ourselves, some seasons are hard, and love can become an afterthought. Time is spent working on everything other than the very relationship God designed us to have (GEN 2:18), and we slip into ungratefulness. Love is a choice. We have the choice to love our husbands every day. That love will shine brightly. For love covers a multitude of sins (1 PET 4:8). You would have probably heard people say, 'I fell out of love' or 'We had grown apart' after a divorce or split from a long relationship. Still, the truth of these statements is that the couple had given up on their relationship. It's funny that some people expect to marry someone, and that person to stay the same forever. We change so much from birth to adolescence and again from adolescence to adulthood. But it doesn't stop there. We are creatures experiencing growth and change as we live and learn. As believers, we can expect great change as we mature in our faith, learn His word, and be more intentional in our lives. Not everyone will change for the better; sometimes, these changes negatively impact our relationships. The unchangeable fact is that all relationships take work. Biblical relationships are paved with hardship, sacrifice, and love. Jesus showed us the ultimate sacrifice for love. He loves us so much; he died for us to save us. John 3:15-16 says:

> *That whosoever believeth in him should not perish, but have eternal life. **For God so loved the world, that he gave his only begotten Son, that whosoever believeth in him should not perish, but have everlasting life.***

God's word is a testament to the work we must put into relationships. The work we do to cultivate relationships is beautiful because it grows and builds us as individuals if we allow it. We must be willing to change and grow to emulate that for our children. Jesus didn't come here as a man. He came as a baby who grew into the man who sacrificed His life for ours. His ministry was all about teaching and connecting with others. He talked with people of all ages regardless of status or sinfulness. He showed unconditional love even to those who would have him killed. We must do the same in our marriage and life. We can't expect to know what to do naturally. We must grow and learn as Jesus did. Understanding that great change and impact takes time. Look at how the life of Jesus has impacted people since his life, death, and resurrection. The promise of his return has brought many people comfort. This, too, is similar to our marriage. It may seem hard and, at times, hopeless or awful, but the beauty is in getting through those hard times and being a better version of ourselves. We can have hope that one day we will look around at the full table before us, with children, grandchildren, and more love than we could have ever hoped for.

We choose to love our husbands because it reflects our love for God, and that love will spread to our children. As a light can brighten the whole room, so we, walking in the spirit, can light our home. Loving our husbands brings peace and beauty into the home that lays the foundation for everything else. We have become *one flesh* with our husbands, so when we are at war with one another, we are at war with ourselves. Mark 3:25 says:

> *And if a house be divided against itself, that house cannot stand.*

Husband and wife run the household. When they are at war the household falls. We must choose love and unity in the home.

SUBMISSION TO ONES HUSBAND

The real issue of unity in the home is leadership.
Someone must lead, of course as Christians, we know
whom; Ephesians 5:22 says:

> *Wives, submit yourself unto your own husbands, as*
> *unto the Lord.*

This verse instructs us toward obedient submission,
respectfully, to one's husband. This is a brief way of
explaining how a woman should treat her husband: The
woman should seek her husband's will (as she does the
LORDS); she shouldn't curiously inquire after his work but
entrust and have faith he is acting in goodness and
righteousness. The woman should take care of her family
affairs and speak to her husband and of her husband
respectfully and becomingly. She is to do all this while
cheerfully, open-heartedly, and lovingly knowing that this
submission is voluntary and pleasing to the LORD (COL
3:18).

Most of us today are triggered by this sentiment
above. To be submissive or obedient to one's husband
conjures pictures in our minds of the 50s housewife with
her pearls and her hip-enhancing pleated skirts, dinner on
the table by five with a cheerful demeanor and a clean house
to match, a well-dressed and preened wife for a husband to
enjoy when he returns from 'bringing home the bacon.'

What a picture. It also conjures thoughts of children sitting respectfully and perfectly at the table, quiet and polite, only speaking when spoken to. Some of this may sound good, but it is also extremely ungodly because, in this picture-perfect home, godliness is not a heart desire; perfection is. Obedience and submission to one's husband doesn't refer to a dictatorship with you as the oppressed biting your tongue, but rather a beautiful kingdom where there is willingness, devotion, partnership, and realization of purpose. You are the Queen in the house of your kingdom, and your actions have far-reaching consequences, however small they may seem. God made us different, men and women, to suit different purposes; it's not that one is better or above the other in importance. It's that we are both created to serve and fulfill different needs.

Generally speaking, a home is not made homely by a man, a guest is not made to feel at home by a man, and children are not softly nurtured by a man. Some may see these as stereotypes, but when we get to the crux of it: Women usually are the talkers, the ones who remember birthdays and names. We connect with people and their lives, becoming a confidante, someone people can weep with and receive empathy from in return. We are emotional, sometimes to our detriment because we feel more than we believe we can handle. But God made us this way. God made us to be emotional, to feel deeply. Men, however, I am sure you would agree, don't always feel this depth of emotion. Sometimes they can seem harsh, hard, or distant. They are well-suited to leadership because their emotions don't usually get in their way as much as with a woman. What of aggression? It's a feeling we've all experienced to one degree or another but tends to occur more commonly in men. Is this bad? Well, it depends first on how we define aggression. If we are talking about senseless violence and hostility, then yes, it is bad, but if by aggression we mean a more subtle feeling that enhances focus and determination but doesn't devolve into an angry tirade, then this is actually a very positive trait, one that even women need from time to time, whether it's mustering the fortitude to finish the dishes after a long day of tantrums or working through the night to finish a project before its deadline. A man's aggressive nature, used in wisdom, turns anger into drive and determination through love, that can help him push through hard work and pain for the needs of his family.

1 Corinthians 9:24-27 says:

Know ye not that they which run in a race run all, but one receiveth the prize? So run, that ye may obtain. And every man that striveth for the mastery is temperate in all things. Now they do it to obtain a corruptible crown; but we an incorruptible. I therefore so run, not as uncertainly; so, fight I, not as one that beateth the air: But I keep under my

body, and bring it into subjection: lest that by any
means, when I have preached to others, I myself
should be a castaway.

The duty of man is providing for his family (1 TIM
5:8), leading and ruling over his household (1 TIM 3:4), and
abounding himself in good works (1 COR 15:58) so he will
not be corrupted by ungodly doings (PSA 1:1-6). These
responsibilities require a certain amount of self-control,
determination, and perseverance that aggression is often
used to achieve. Aggression alone without placement is just
anger. Anger degrades to its stronger form of wrath; when
unchecked and unused, will only lead to evil doing (PSA
37:8, PRO 3:27)

FEMINISM FREE MARRIAGE

God knew that man needed a companion, so he
made us. Genesis 2:18 says:

And the LORD God said, It is not good that the man
should be alone; I will make him an help meet for
him.

I am sure you have heard, 'Behind every great man,
there's a great woman.' This is not from the bible, of course,
but was an old saying that became popular during the
feminist movement in the 1960s/70s; sadly, the intention of
the phrase was a call for attention, a selfish desire to be

known. It fuelled an onslaught of self-righteousness and pride; Pop artists and icons furthered the feminist cause with words and lyrics that spoke of women coming out of the kitchen and making a name for themselves. I think for many women the main trigger word is behind.

In the song 'Sisters are Doing it for Themselves' the Eurythmics said:

> *Now there was a time When they used to say That behind every great man There had to be a great woman But in these times of change You know that it's no longer true So we're comin' out of the kitchen 'Cause there's somethin' we forgot to say to you, we say Sisters are doin' it for themselves Standin' on their own two feet And ringin' on their own bells, we say Sisters are doin' it for themselves.*

If we consider what was happening at the time, this makes sense, as men were turning away from God, faith, and the church, yet still expecting the same devotion and obedience from their wives as the men before them. The lyrics "The inferior sex got a new exterior, We got doctors, lawyers, politicians too," came later in the song. In many ways, these lines suggested that motherhood and homemaking were equated with being in the kitchen, and this work was considered inferior to the work of doctors, lawyers, and politicians. This was effective propaganda at the time and led many women to desire stepping out of the home and into the 'glory' of the world. The line "ringin' on their own bells" signifies that women were no longer serving men but were now serving themselves. What ended up happening was a hell of a lot of women miserably working in offices and jobs away from their homes and children, feeling less fulfilled as they did less-meaningful tasks, while at the same time filling the pockets of Men who utilised the extra labour for their gain. Nowadays, we have less children per family, and most families require two working parents leaving the children at the hands of the state for most of the day. I'm all for women working if that is what they're called to do. Woman should be allowed to work outside of the home including married women and mothers, but I don't believe that normalising this while their children are in daycare is helpful for our society.

A husband and wife rely on each other. A woman who takes care of her home and children is an important part of a well-working family unit. With both parents working it is hard to keep a well-balanced home. Many women crave earthly praise, but we have been given the greatest gift, the gift of everlasting life; because of this we can live a life where we wholeheartedly live for God, our husbands, and our children, serving them to the greatest of our abilities. In that servitude, greatness is accomplished, light is shone on our husband, glorifying him for his leadership and inevitably shining a light on God and our savior who died so that we could live. When we do as God commands it pleases Him. This kind of servitude, this kind of love, is one we mothers should want for our daughters; it is the service of one who loves deeply and rejoices in her God-given tasks, no matter their appearance or outcome. We can be joyful when we make sure our hearts are in the right place. When our hearts are with God.

God never meant for women to be seen as lesser beings. Throughout human history, people have done things out of alignment with God and what He meant for us. Galatians 3:28 says:

> *There is neither Jew nor Greek, there is neither bond nor free, there is neither male nor female: for ye are all one in Christ Jesus.*

It was revolutionary, although at times within society, we as women have been treated as lesser, it was not the design for us by our creator. Paul makes it clear that we are all one in Christ; gender nor ethnicity matters in relation to salvation. The fallen nature of humanity and our desire to sin have led us, over and over again, into times of disrespect and desecration. Men are now being emasculated and vilified to serve the purposes of the devil, in order to disarm and subjugate us. We are being fed the lie that we are oppressed by the patriarchy. In reality, our true adversary is playing us. The devil is trying to divide and conquer us. He uses fear as a weapon. We must arm ourselves with truth; we don't need feminism to be seen as equal, to be respected, or to have purpose. God has given us all these things; we only need to listen to the Spirit, to God. One of our God-given purposes is to be a helper for Adam, for our husbands.

HUSBANDS DUTY

Husbands are also called to behave in a certain way toward their wives. However, before I delve into this topic, know that this is not meant as an exhortation for you to hold over your husband, but rather to help you grow in love and wisdom on your journey to becoming a Titus 2 Mother. Colossians 3:19 says:

Husbands, love your wives, and be not bitter against them.

Paul calls husbands to be gentle and loving toward their wives. Bitterness causes contention and upset. Most of us have had experiences with our husbands where we might have been upset about something he said to us or the manner in which he treated us. That state of being upset can sometimes lead to arguments and a flippant use of the tongue. When a man acts in a way that is bitter or harsh, he shows a lack of self-control and meekness. Self-control is something that makes us, as women, feel safe and secure both in our relationships and in real-world situations where there are actual dangers. It's understandable that we might be concerned, yet we must also bite our tongues and not throw stones. Ephesians 5:22-33 says:

> *Wives, submit yourselves unto your own husbands, as unto the Lord. For the husband is the head of the wife, even as Christ is the head of the church: and he is the saviour of the body. Therefore as the church is subject unto Christ, so let the wives be to their own husbands in every thing. Husbands, love your wives, even as Christ also loved the church, and gave himself for it; That he might sanctify and cleanse it with the washing of water by the word, That he might present it to himself a glorious church, not having spot, or wrinkle, or any such thing; but that it should be holy and without blemish. So ought men to love their wives as their own bodies. He that loveth his wife loveth himself. For no man ever yet hated his own flesh; but nourisheth and cherisheth it, even as the Lord the church: For we are members of his body, of his flesh, and of his bones. For this cause shall a man leave his father and mother, and shall be joined unto his wife, and they two shall be one flesh. This is a great mystery: but I speak concerning Christ and the church. Nevertheless let every one of you in*

*particular so love his wife even as himself; and the
wife see that she reverence her husband.*

Here, Paul likens the husband to Christ, as Christ
was the head of the church, so is the husband the head of his
wife. The husband is a leader, tasked with leading his wife
and family. This leadership is to be performed in love. Just
as Christ loved us so much that he died for us, the husband
is encouraged to love his wife in the same manner, loving
her as himself.

In the verses above, Paul is discussing the concept
of biblical oneness with our husbands and Christ, which
brings forth ideas worthy of discussion. Upon reading these
verses, I began to realize the importance of having love,
whether it's towards God, our neighbor, or even ourselves.
Once married, a woman is one with her husband. If we
don't have love for ourselves, how can we wholeheartedly
love our husbands, who are now a part of us? This
realization impacted me greatly as I had disliked myself for
a long time. I found my voice annoying, and I wished to be
someone else. I loathed the gifts I clearly possessed because
they reminded me of my childhood origins. Sometimes, the
barrier in our relationships is simply our own dislike for
ourselves. While I'm not advocating that we spend all our
time selfishly loving ourselves, as that would be a call to
vanity, it's important to realize that if we dislike ourselves,
we will: one, focus inwardly and are more likely to give in

to selfish desires, and two, hold hate in our hearts which we will spread. We must remember that we are IN christ and He is IN us, and at the very least, not hate ourselves but have love through faith. He is doing His work through us, and we must remember not to judge His work by our own subjective standards but to have FAITH in His plans through us, knowing that God, being perfect, will not break His promises and will never leave or forsake us (HEB 13:5.)

OUR ROLE

What we model for our children also serves as a model for the world. Our marriage should inspire younger women to emulate and desire such qualities within their own marriages. We are instructed to take actions that will assist, allow, or help cultivate emotional stability and depth in marriage. As mothers, we can be certain that we are modeling what a mother and wife should be for our children. Unfortunately, when we behave inappropriately, we implicitly condone such behaviors in the eyes of our children. Here are some questions to help us remain mindful: Would I want my daughter to act this way? Would I want my son to have a wife who treats him in this manner? If the answer to these questions is no, then change is necessary...

TAKE AWAYS

- Submission to our husbands is voluntary and should be something we can find joy in doing, knowing we are serving the LORD.
- Men and women have distinct roles and must play to the strengths God has given in order to function faithfully and harmoniously.
- Women are emotional, which makes us less able to lead on average and better able to connect, nurture, and strengthen the community.

HEART PROBING QUESTIONS

1. Do I treat my husband with respect and honor?
2. Am I modeling the right behaviors for my children?
3. Are there ways my husband and I can improve our relationship to better prepare our children for relationships and marriage?
4. Do I acknowledge that I love myself?
5. Have I taken on any feminist views of marriage?

CHAPTER 8

Love Your Children

To love our children is to share our time with them. Time is the most valuable resource we have on earth, and it is one we must spend with our children. In the thirteenth century, The Frederick Experiment was conducted. The experiment involved taking babies from their mothers and placing them in the care of a nurse. These nurses were instructed to meet the babies' physical needs without talking or interacting with them. The purpose was to determine if language was an innate ability and to discover man's original language. Frederick II was curious to see if the infants would speak Greek, Hebrew, or some other dialect.

In the end the experiment was cut short due to babies dying. According to the documentation they did attempt to return the babies who survived the initial round of deaths during the experiment, but they too died shortly after returning to their mothers. Dr Ornish declared that "You must love and be loved in order to survive." He explains: "The scientific evidence… leaves little doubt that love and intimacy are powerful determinants of our health and survival. Why they have such an impact remains somewhat a mystery" (Dean Ornish, Love and Survival, p. 22). Dr Ornish then concluded: "Mystery remains. No one can fully explain . . . why love and intimacy matter so much" (on p. 171). But we can explain it. We were made in His image (GEN 1:27). And "God is love" 1 John 4:16 says:

> *And we have known and believed the love that God hath to us. God is love; and he that dwelleth in love dwelleth in God, and God in him.*

Ornish summarizes the rapidly accumulating body of data by saying: "Anything that promotes feelings of love and intimacy is healing; anything that promotes isolation, separation, loneliness, loss, hostility, anger, cynicism, depression, alienation, and related feelings often leads to suffering, disease, and premature death from all causes" (Love and Survival, p. 29). We humans need love, and God provides us with love in abundance. Until our children are able to fully understand this, we are the bridge – the loving embodiment of God on Earth for our children, just as Jesus Christ is for us.

Jesus shows us the importance of giving our children time when he made time for them. Luke 18:15-17 says:

> *And they brought unto him also infants, that he would touch them: but when his disciples saw it, they rebuked them. But Jesus called them unto him, and said, Suffer little children to come unto me, and forbid them not: for of such is the kingdom of God. Verily I say unto you, Whosoever shall not receive the kingdom of God as a little child shall in no wise enter therein.*

Jesus, amidst healing the sick, blind, and crippled, made time for the children. He told his disciples, when they rebuked him, to let the children come to him, saying that only those who receive the kingdom like children will enter. Perhaps you, like me, have felt like a child as you parent your children or as you come to the LORD on bent knees in complete overwhelm and dismay. No matter our age, there is still a childlike nature within all of us. We learn and grow, but our short lives are nothing compared to the eternal. Loving our children allows them and us to glimpse into the holy love God, our Father in heaven, has for us—an unconditional, eternal love.

We can doubt ourselves and our abilities as parents when the behavior of our children creates chaos, but it's important to note that this is an opportunity and an indication for us to help guide our children. It's in those testing attitudes or tantrums that we can seize the moment to deal with a heart issue. Sometimes issues arise that we were oblivious to. Other times we have to deal with the same issue time and time again until the day something "clicks" or a new level of comprehension and understanding is reached. My eldest son, on occasion, has shocked me with his attitude as he tried to push the boundaries. He's eight and like most kids, eager to try new things. In this, he can learn, grow, and accomplish something new, and this is usually something children do naturally, with joy. We can think of a baby learning to walk, for example; they don't quit the first few times they fall over but continue trying day after day until they can walk. We, as humans, tend to want to test our limits too. We can look at athletes, extreme sports professionals, and adventurers like Steve Irwin, Bear Grylls, and Wim Hof to get a glimpse of how far some people are willing to go to push their bodies and minds to the limit.

For my eldest son, it's all about missions. If we set him a task, he is excited and wants to see how well he can accomplish it. Currently, he's learning to cook, he's writing a novel, and he's got the mission of putting the laundry on the line. Some tasks may seem silly or maybe too big for an eight-year-old, but he is interested in doing these things to further his own skills and abilities. Challenges are healthy; they give your child a chance to take on responsibilities as both an individual and as part of the family unit. One of our biggest tasks as parents is to help them become independent. Sometimes they just need you to give them responsibility. Failure is just a lesson waiting to be learned and understood. This is something we teach our children: 'Roussel's never give up.' Training our children before they're fully grown is paramount if we wish to raise capable adults who can be launched out of our homes and into the world.

BE FRUITFUL AND MULTIPLY

Most women, no matter their beliefs, feel a craving to have babies. Even after labouring and delivering, as soon as that baby's in arms, there is this emptiness in the womb that begs to be filled. Genesis 1:28 says:

> *And God blessed them, and God said unto them, Be fruitful, and multiply, and replenish the earth, and subdue it: and have dominion over the fish of the sea, and over the fowl of the air, and over every living thing that moveth upon the earth.*

The instruction here is clear: have babies, many babies, and that doing so is fruitful and good. As a woman who started off without faith, I can tell you that pregnancies were horrendous. My thoughts and feelings focused firmly on the negatives of childbearing. 'It's uncomfortable, it's painful, it's torture, it's like having a parasite that is living inside you, stealing all that you need from within.' These thoughts were acceptable and validated among friends, family, and influencers online. You would think that with this kind of mindset, the last thing I would want is another child. However, this was untrue. I had two children out of faith, the first in hospital and the second at home, and I still wanted more. With my first three pregnancies, I can recall being uncomfortable and annoyed about pregnancy, but the pains of labor itself were forgotten once I had my baby in my arms. I think John 16:21-22 speaks volumes to these sentiments of joy after childbirth:

> *A woman when she is in travail hath sorrow, because her hour has come: but as soon as she is delivered of the child, she remembereth no more the anguish, for the joy that a man is born into the world. And ye now therefore have sorrow: but I will see you again, and your heart shall rejoice, and your joy no man taketh away from you.*

Here Jesus tells us the beauty that is childbearing, He compares the anguish of childbirth to the misery His death will bring; and a mother's joy of holding her newborn child, with that of His follower's joy upon seeing him again, resurrected. We see here the importance, the significance of new human life. We are to treasure it, be joyous in it.

REDEMPTIVE EXPERIENCE

I don't think I truly understood joy until I had Grace, my fourth living child. That's not to say I wasn't joyful for my other children; it's just that her birth held a different meaning. Her birth was a completely redemptive experience. My husband and I lost two babies to miscarriage before we fell pregnant with her, and those losses brought many changes to our family. The biggest change was in me. I felt broken after I lost our first baby. I sat in depression for some time before I couldn't face it anymore. I felt called to speak with other women to hear their stories and gain some understanding of how to deal with this monstrosity of grief. The Joy of Sunflowers Podcast was born; I have spoken with over a hundred women to date. The beautiful women I have spoken to and continue to speak to share their hearts with me. I weep with some and laugh with others, and in every conversation, love shines through even the darkest of places. They love their babies. They're babies that were, in many cases, never born on Earth but are loved all the same. This taught me that the pain and grief were something I could let go of while still loving, cherishing, and honoring my heaven babies.

Speaking to so many women about loss and delivery and taking our previous experiences with midwives and doctors into account, we felt confident that with God we could do a better job of delivering our baby into the world. So, we chose to have a freebirth. Grace was born on 19th June 2023 in the bathroom of our off-grid farm cottage, with a gymnastic-style entrance. She came into the world, into her father's hands, and then into mine. It was my husband and I, some candles, a warm fire, worship music, and our three other children who decided to get out of bed just as I was entering the final stages of labor. Grace greeted us calmly at 2.8kg and 49cm long, the tiniest baby I had ever birthed. The birthing experience was beautiful, and it is what so many women pray for after loss. It felt as if this was my redeeming childbirth. I praised God so much during and after labor. The first words I spoke to her were, 'Thank you for being alive.'

VALUE OF LIFE

My experience of pregnancy, loss, and redemption has taught me so much about the blessing and miracle of a child. There really is no guarantee of having living children. Before we had Grace, I already thought children were important, but after her, I felt and knew it to be true. I have thanked God and praised Him constantly since for all of my children, including the ones I have the hope of meeting in heaven. There have been these moments of overwhelming joy and gratitude that both my husband and I have experienced with our baby Grace and older children. Psalm 127:3-5 comes to mind in those moments; it says:

> *Lo, children are an heritage of the LORD: and the fruit of the womb is his reward. As arrows are in the hand of a mighty man; so are children of the youth. Happy is the man that hath his quiver full of them: they shall not be ashamed, but they shall speak with the enemies in the gate.*

Psalm 127 is entitled "A Song of Degrees for Solomon." Here, we find sentiments about childbearing that are very different from those of today's society, where people often have children past thirty only to place them in childcare to avoid interrupting their lifestyle. (This is not referring to everyone, as some people come from homes where both parents have to work, or perhaps one parent may even be divorced or single.) Psalm 127 tells us that children aren't just products of our biology but are a beautiful blessing from the LORD and should be treated as such. It also states that a happy man will have many children. As women, mothers, and wives, dedicated to helping our husbands, we can be sure that we find happiness in the fullness of our roles, in knowledge of obeying God and our husbands. This verse also shows that, envisioning many children, we can presume that there are many boys and girls. Those boys were raised to assist their fathers in labor, becoming a delight to him through the easing of hardship. Likewise, daughters became helping hands for their mothers until they too were married, enriching the family culture with a multi-generational church, tribe, or community. I picture this for my future. I pray for it. Do you? To have a long table full of my children and their spouses, and then the garden full of their children running around. Everyone happy to be there and be part of the festivities that occur so regularly because we want them to.

BURDENS OF SOCIETY

Society would have us believe that children are a burden and that having a large family is a sure way toward misery. We have women shouting out 'my body, my choice,' willing to kill the most vulnerable people in our society so they don't have to be parents. When I first went through a miscarriage, I had to wrap my head around the fact that I had truly lost something. Society told me it was 'just a clump of cells' not worthy of the identity of a baby, but God told us differently. Jeremiah 1:5 says:

> *Before I formed thee in the belly I knew thee; and before thou camest forth out of the womb I sanctified thee, and I ordained thee a prophet unto the nations.*

If you have lost babies, take comfort here. God knew them. They were born into heaven, and one day we will be reunited with them. We truly lost someone. I laugh at the clump of cells argument now because we are all a clump of cells; we are made up of many cells. There is no shying away from the truth. We also have science that shows the light that sparks when an egg is fertilized. The literal light of life occurs at conception. Most scientists will tell you that life begins at conception. It's about what is deemed worthy of life, rights, and love that is argued. For us Christians, there is no argument; we have the truth: Matthew 25:40 says:

> *And the King shall answer and say unto them, Verily I say unto you, Inasmuch as ye have done it unto one of the least of these my brethren, ye have done it unto me.*

Although this is referring to how we treat those who are sick and needy, I believe this also speaks to the unborn and their protection. They have no voice outside of the womb, yet they're being silenced completely. They are being thrown away. Abortion, birth control, and the morning-after pill try to position women to see the unborn as something disposable, a problem to be remedied. I've spoken to over a hundred people about pregnancy loss, and I have learned that everyone, even those who choose to abort, hurt after their baby dies. We know we have lost something, and no amount of belittling can change the truth of the matter. Life is sacred, and the life of the unborn is the most sacred of all. Jesus developed in the womb and was born from the water of the womb just like every child. His coming brought hope and love to people. Jesus blessed people and healed them of their ailments, and in his death, freed us all from sin. There were people born throughout the days of the Bible who were key to Jesus's coming and to the stories that are so powerful and healing to millions today.

We cannot know how each child will grow or the impact they'll have on the world. The only certain thing is that God has a plan for them, and his plans are greater than ours (ISA 55:8-10). As I watch my children grow and see myself changing in faith, I am constantly reminded of the children's book "The Three Trees" by Angela Elwell Hunt/ David C. Cook, which speaks of three trees who have dreams of being different things: one a treasure box, one a boat for kings, and the other wishes to grow big and tall pointing toward God. Of course, their dreams are dashed when three men come to chop them down. I won't spoil the entire story, but I will tell you that the tree who wanted to be a treasure box ended up being an animal trough and was in despair by the outcome until a baby was placed into the trough. The most precious treasure that ever lived: the baby Jesus. This story greatly illustrates that even if we cannot see the path before us and the meaning behind what we face, He has a plan, and He sees where it is we are headed. Romans 8:28 says:

> *And we know that all things work together for good to them that love God, to them who are the called according to his purpose.*

These are things we can take joy in and have faith in, knowing that God has a plan and will lead and guide us. When we seek Him and do our best to obey, we can help in His great plan. When we model this for our children through our prayers for them and our actions toward and around them, they too can see the beauty and wonders of God.

NURTURING THEIR GIFTS

Teaching is not always a simple task. One must have a teachable heart in order for teaching to be effective. Many people view teaching as burdensome being that children can get very hyped up and easily distracted. Proverbs 22:6 says:

> *Train up a child in the way he should go: and when he is old he will not depart from it.*

This verse speaks volumes, not just in respect to God's word but also in all other teachings. I also find comfort in it because when we teach our children skills that will help them build confidence and independence, we also ensure help for the future. God's word instructs us to honor, respect, and love our parents (EXO 20:12), and in that, we are obliged to help them when they need it (1 TIM 5:8). It is not just a mere responsibility but something we want to do when brought up with nurturing praise and competency. It's our responsibility as God-given authorities and teachers of our children to teach them.

Imagine your daughter joyously helping you in all things baby-related, getting diapers and wipes, bottles, or preparing baby food. Your daughter can be a great asset to you, one you can trust to delegate tasks to if you show her and train her in the ways of motherhood, giving her an understanding of the role's importance and significance in God's kingdom.

It isn't a chore for them but a great honor where they feel glad to be helping. Children want to be part of the running of the home; they want to feel a sense of belonging and importance, and as if they're needed, just like we do. Motherhood isn't just an instruction from the LORD but a blessing and honor to grow His kingdom and cultivate the kinds of characteristics that shine a light for others to Him. We can show our daughters the joy of children by having children, taking care of them, teaching them, and spending time diligently preparing lessons, materials, meals, and the home. We inspire the desire for childbearing through our actions and attitudes toward our work as mothers. We are called to love our children, and that love should show as care, contentment, gratitude, and joy. Know that with all the work you do now, the time you spend diligently teaching, one day will be replayed to you in your child's actions, and the attitude you showed while teaching will show on their face.

When Jesus came here, he didn't just tell us how to be; he showed us. He led his disciples and the people who followed him. He spoke many words of wisdom (MAT 5), but he also worked to heal the sick, show compassion for the hurt, and give love to all, even those who would have him killed (JHN 10:24-30, LUK 23:34).

Loving our children and taking our time to teach them, love them, and bring them up in truth is something we are asked to do Deuteronomy 6:7 says:

> *And thou shalt teach them diligently unto thy children, and shalt talk of them when thou sittest in thine house, and when thou walkest by the way, and when thou liest down, and when thou risest up.*

Here, the importance of passing on passionate and steadfast faith is stressed to parents. We are to see this task as one of importance because it is one of the many ways God brings His children to Him. We are called to teach our children so that they too can walk in faith.

God wants our children with Him (3 JHN 1:4), just as much as He wants us with Him. He loves us. God uses our teachings to soften the hearts of our children and our own hearts. When we make teaching our children important, God is made important in our home. I see so many people go to church, and that's it for their worship for the week, besides saying grace at the table. Once a week for a couple of hours doesn't sound like a lifelong committed relationship to me. To love our children, we need to love Him. We model love for our children by showing them the love we have for them and our Father in heaven.

In Titus 2:4, we are told to love our children. Loving is not hard to do, even when you are exhausted or feeling underappreciated, if you are grateful for the children God has blessed you with. I can safely say that I am incredibly grateful, and I do not take the miracle that is my children's lives for granted...

TAKEAWAYS

- We must love our children.
- We can love our children no matter the hardship as long as we are grateful for the blessing and miracle that this child is ours and alive.
- We can hold many emotions, like sadness, and still feel overwhelming joy.
- Sparing our children from discipline is not helpful to our child's development.
- Teaching our children isn't always easy but it is rewarding.

HEART PROBING QUESTIONS

1. Do you take moments to relish in gratitude for the children you have?
2. Have you told your children what they mean to you?
3. Are your children aware of what God's word says about children and their importance?
4. Have you taken on unbiblical parenting methods?
5. Are you disciplining your children?

CHAPTER 9

Be Chaste and Discreet

To be discreet means exercising self-restraint and showing prudence in speech and behavior. On the other hand, Etiquette relies on practices prescribed by cultural norms and authorities within society. Both impact our behavior, but only one requires us to conform to the world. Throughout humanity, we have seen civilizations become morally corrupt; we've watched people turn away from God and become obsessed with money, power, and status. As Christians, we cannot follow the world. There is a degree of fitting in to spread the gospel, but there are also moments where we must stand out. Like Daniel, who continued praying even though it meant he would go into the lion's den; or like David, who stepped forward to fight Goliath when no one else would; or like Esther, who went to the king to save her people when she hadn't been summoned; or like Moses, who stood before Pharaoh and demanded he set the Israelites free. We cannot conform to the same speech and dress code of those around us if it goes against what God wants or calls us to do.

BEING DISCREET IN SOCIETY

Now more than ever, we need to use discernment and be discreet in our public presence. Lately, I have been reading and listening to old books with my children, such as Little Women and Little House in the Big Woods. Upon reading such books, it is hard not to compare the social etiquette of their time to ours. Suppose a person was unhappy with their life or did something unfavorable. In that case, they might confide in only those closest to them, or they risked being the 'talk of the town' and ruining their own reputation, as well as the reputation of their family. Social blunders could be the difference between having security in marriage, finding work, or becoming a burden. At that time, this choice would usually be permanent.

Nowadays, people are rewarded for their blunders, showing the worst and darkest versions of themselves in a bid to be relatable. Comments, likes, shares, and follows have become a new currency that comes at a great cost. The game of who can get the most attention is being played, and countless people are vying for first place, but there are no winners. For many people, there is a desire to be seen, and social media feeds that desire.

Being discreet is not about being heartless or pretending that everything is okay. It is about safeguarding the hearts around you, including your own. It is easy for us to take to a social platform, post something that we know will be relatable to others, and have them pander to our desire to be loved and seen, but it will not give us what we truly want or crave. It will not give us the unconditional love of the Father or the abundant joy that is felt when we think of being in His arms, reunited with Him in heaven. Matthew 11:28-29 says:

> *Come unto me, all ye that labour and are heavy laden, and I will give you rest. Take my yoke upon you, and learn of me; for I am meek and lowly in heart: and ye shall find rest unto your souls.*

Here, Jesus encourages us to rest in him. We don't have to suffer silently or alone. When we voice our concerns in prayer, we can release the burden of worry and anxiety, handing it to Him, knowing that His plans are better than ours. (JER 29:11.) Psalm 55:22 says:

> *Cast thy burden upon the LORD, and he shall*
> *sustain thee: he shall never suffer the righteous to*
> *be moved.*

Here, we are told to give our troubles to God. David often mentions these sentiments in his songs, like in Psalms 46:1-3 where he speaks of God as our refuge and reminds us that God is always with us.

BEING DISCREET IN THE COMMUNITY

As a community of believers, we are to help our brothers and sisters constructively and lift them up in love, Galatians 6:1-5 says:

> *Brethren, if a man be overtaken in a fault, ye which*
> *are spiritual, restore such an one in the spirit of*
> *meekness; considering thyself, lest thou also be*
> *tempted. Bear ye one another's burdens, and so fulfil*
> *the law of Christ. For if a man think himself to be*
> *something, when he is nothing, he deceiveth himself.*
> *But let every man prove his own work, and then*
> *shall he have rejoicing in himself alone, and not in*
> *another. For every man shall bear his own burden.*

Here, Paul exhorts believers to edify each other. Therefore, we should remind ourselves to help those in Christ with their burdens and with the strengthening of their faith. Spiritually mature believers (those strong in their faith) are encouraged to assist new or weak believers. We're meant to be a community that comes together when a fellow brother or sister needs leadership, spiritual strength, and intervention. Here, Paul also says that every man should bear his own burdens and rejoice in his own work alone. This isn't to say we cannot ask for help, share what we have learnt or what we are having issues with, there are times when it is good to share our grievances with others. For example, Paul, in Romans 7, shares about his struggles with the flesh. Romans 7:15 says:

> *For that which I do I allow not: for what I would, that do I not ; but what I hate, that I do.*

Paul shares his struggles not to burden his brethren but to edify them in truth. While others might shy away from the light and speak lies, claiming they don't sin, Paul's humble nature encourages us to acknowledge the truth, reveal our shortcomings earnestly, and understand that these actions are of the flesh. Therefore, a light can shine on our sin, making it easier to apply correction and change through faith. Paul shows them that the mind and the flesh are different, and though he is saved and his mind serves the Lord, his flesh serves the law of sin (ROM 7:25).

Like Paul, we must use discernment in our speech regarding sharing our struggles with others. If we look to

Paul's writings, he always considers the purpose of what is being said, not attempting to present an autobiography to the hearer. Similarly, if we're going to share our own faults to edify others, we should still take care to speak in a way that might be edifying, like Paul. To put it simply, we still need to take great care with our speech, not leaving our tongue unbridled with every thought. Now, if it is us who are in need of edification, then we should first go to God in faith, knowing He will never leave us nor forsake us, and then to others in Christ. However, we must still use discernment in conduct, in speech, and in regard to whom we speak to, knowing that God is the only perfect judge and counselor.

WHEN UNHAPPY WITH OUR HUSBANDS AND OTHER PEOPLE

When parents openly disagree in front of their children, it creates chaos in the home. Children, perhaps subconsciously, can use these moments of disagreement to manipulate the softer of the two parents. In our family's case, I tend to be the softer one. So, we have adopted the 'united front' approach and will try our best to discuss things when the children are asleep. It is worth noting that when we, as wives, disobey our husbands, choosing to try and usurp their authority, we only fuel discomfort and a disobedient nature within our children. If this is a hard pill to swallow, think back to times when you fought with your husband in front of your children, and then recall the behavior of your children both immediately after and the next day. We can most likely recall misbehavior and unhelpful attitudes. Sometimes a discussion must be had. We cannot always have the perfect circumstances, with our children in bed and everyone else out of earshot. Life happens and, in those moments or seasons, we need to do our best to be calm and discuss issues instead of shouting about them. I went through a time of feeling guilty for our occasional arguments in front of the children, but I realized they are a window into marriage and a demonstration of the work the Spirit is doing within us, as we argue less and instead have reasonable discussions.

We have also begun to make time to discuss our plans for each week so we can be on the same page and know what's ahead. Sometimes the root cause of arguments is simply the unease that comes with not knowing what is going on. These discussions may also include any issues or grievances we have with each other or the children. Here, we allow each of us to have a voice unhindered by the other. If you find you are speaking over each other, a great tool is a speaking stick, binder, or pen. So, whoever is speaking can hold it and put it down when finished, then and only then can the other person talk. I know this may sound ridiculous and something out of a kindergarten class, but desperate times call for desperate measures. If you're at the point where you're scared to speak or feel attacked when spoken to, you'll only fuel more animosity, discontent, and resentment toward each other if you continue as you are.

Sometimes, we mothers can feel that our husbands do not listen, are too harsh with us and our children, and are unwilling to change and grow. But the truth is, we don't know. We don't know what is in their heads and how close they are to a big change or revelation, which will have them speaking more cautiously to their children and to us. 1 Peter 3:1-5 says:

> *Likewise, ye wives, **be in subjection to your own husbands; that, if any obey not the word, they also may without the word be won by the conversation of the wives; While they behold your chaste conversation **coupled** with fear. Whose adorning let it not be that outward **adorning** of plaiting the hair, and of wearing of gold, or of putting on of apparel; But **let it be** the hidden man of the heart, in that which is not corruptible, **even the ornament** of a meek and quiet spirit, which is in the sight of God of great price. For after this manner in the old time the holy women also, who trusted in God, adorned themselves, being in subjection unto their own husbands:*

Peter implies that a wife's respectful and pure conduct has the potential to strengthen and lead her husband to faith in Christ, even when he is a non-believer. The idea is that husbands will see the difference in their wives' behavior and will attribute that change and growth to Christ, deeming that faith is the cause of her change. We are to obey God above all, and in doing so, we show a single-minded devotion to Christ. We show our husbands our reverence for God and how our faith contributes to our submission to Him.

Often, lacking the ability to be discreet is a symptom of a bigger problem: pride or self-righteousness. We act as if the other person is a sinner, and we aren't. We can search within ourselves and remember that we all sin and fall short of the glory of God (ROM 3:23) and that Jesus taught us that as sinners, we should not condemn others for their sins, John 8:1-12 says:

> *Jesus went unto the mount of Olives. And early in the morning he came again into the temple, and all the people came unto him; and he sat down, and taught them. And the scribes and Pharisees brought unto him a woman taken in adultery; and when they had set her in the midst, They say unto him, Master, this woman was taken in adultery, in the very act. Now Moses in the law commanded us, that such should be stoned: but what sayest thou? This they*

said, tempting him, that they might have to accuse him. But Jesus stooped down, and with his finger wrote on the ground, as though he heard them not. So when they continued asking him, he lifted up himself, and said unto them, He that is without sin among you, let him first cast a stone at her. And again he stooped down, and wrote on the ground. And they which heard it, being convicted by their own conscience, went out one by one, beginning at the eldest, even unto the last: and Jesus was left alone, and the woman standing in the midst. When Jesus had lifted up himself, and saw none but the woman, he said unto her, Woman, where are those thine accusers? hath no man condemned thee? She said, No man, Lord. And Jesus said unto her, Neither do I condemn thee: go, and sin no more. Then spake Jesus again unto them, saying, I am the light of the world: he that followeth me shall not walk in darkness, but shall have the light of life.

In this passage, we can remind ourselves not to get self-righteously angry at fellow sinners, sentencing them to death like the Pharisees. We must love and talk with them in the spirit as Jesus would. He told the accused woman that he did not condemn her. I have seen a great many women take to social media in anger, attacking people who are sinning in the world. The problem isn't that the sin is being addressed; it's that the language used isn't working through love to bring people to Christ. It's used to justify hatred towards another. This reveals a hypocrisy in the attitude of Christians towards the unsaved and can become a stumbling block to them. We need to tap into the meekness God wants for us and embrace the Spirit to nurture and cultivate beauty and life in the world.

WHEN WE ARE DISCONTENT

We can easily become discontent when we are listening and speaking into the daily murmurings of the world. (PHI 2:14) Christian women can be a force of nature and a warrior for God in the world, Proverbs 31:25-26 says:

> *Strength and honour are her clothing; and she shall rejoice in time to come. She openeth her mouth with wisdom; and in her tongue is the law of kindness.*

Here we are told that a virtuous woman is recognized by her strength and dignity. She will act with integrity, respond with faith in God, and be faithful to her family. We should discuss our relationship with our husbands privately. This is to avoid unwanted opinions, callus treatments toward our husband, and bad counsel. At times, I have complained about my husband's actions and gotten some rather ungodly advice in return, as well as having that person vilify my husband. This diminishes our husband's authority in our minds; it gives us justification for our grievances and fosters self-righteous pride. We become the gossiper, the face of ridicule and judgment. As Christian women, how can we expect to lead our daughters when we are fanning the flames of discord within our own homes?

WHEN WE ARE DISCONTENT WITH OUR CHILDREN

If you speak to someone about your children and their behavior, you willingly allow this person to give parenting advice and openly judge or critique your child and parenting. It's important to note that not all advice is created equal. There is good, bad, and very ugly advice. Good advice is a rare thing that, when received, can be a God send, but lousy advice will linger around you like a bad smell; it can sometimes become toxic and choke out the goodness that you may have worked hard to cultivate. When we discuss our children in front of them, they take in what we are saying. If someone speaks ill of them, we should do our best to defend our child, especially if the comments are unwarranted. God has given us someone to discuss the issues we may be facing with our children: our husbands. If we choose to talk to others, we must understand that they have no authority and no real responsibility; their advice, if taken, may have dire consequences. Consequences they will never have to deal with; only you and your husband will bear the burden of following bad counsel and potentially leading your children astray.

CHASTE IN SOCIETY

Married or not, being chaste is for all of us. Being chaste is abstaining from extramarital or all sexual intercourse. Now, this first part, abstaining from unmarried sex, is very much a biblical desire, but abstaining from one's husband is not. The main drive behind this is purity. Hebrews 13:4 says:

> Marriage is honourable in all, and the bed undefiled: but whoremongers and adulterers God will judge.

When you are intimate with your husband your intimacy is not seen as unclean because, marital sex is undefiled. Paul urges believers to marry if they cannot stay celibate. He also tells believers it is better in his opinion not to be married at all and to focus solely on God. Of course, today it's harder than ever to stay celibate with things like porn being accessible at the touch of a button. Even advertisements at the shops and up on billboards often feature inappropriate imagery of scantily clad men or women in a bid to sell a product.

GLORIFIED HARLOT

1 Corinthians 6:16 says:

What? know ye not that he which is joined to an harlot is one body? for two, saith he, shall be one flesh.

Once upon a time, women who 'slept around' were seen as harlots. Terms such as this rendered these particular women dirty, unclean, and unfit for the sanctity of marriage. Much of the thought behind this was that no man wanted to share his wife with another man. While there are a whole range of issues that stem from this, one such issue, in a time before DNA testing, would be that if a woman was suspected to not be a virgin and a man married her and had children, there would be no way to ensure the children were his.

My husband was sadly not my first intimate relationship. As a non-religious teenage girl, I didn't see the harm in it. I was told I should know a man before I married him (the philosophy of the world), and at the age of fifteen, I thought I knew and would marry the boy I was dating. Sadly, the experience left a scar. I realized I wasn't ready, but saying the word 'No!' did little to change the result of the event. I wish I had been more prepared, but I wasn't. Later, my now husband, who was also not Christian at the time, approached the boy about what had happened (we were all in high school), and the boy claimed he was unaware that his advances that day were unwanted. He was very ashamed and apologetic to me afterward. It's awful to think that my experience pales in comparison to so many other teenage girls and women who have been taken advantage of because they willingly and/or naively put themselves in vulnerable situations. (Of course, I absolutely need to mention that there are circumstances where awful things happen, unwarranted and without purposely putting oneself in any particularly bad situation.) I came from a time where the idea of a woman sleeping around had become glorified. Women were shouting out the rhetoric 'If the men can sleep around and be seen as champions, why can't we?' More and more, I saw young girls turning away from the idea of marriage and running into the arms of carnal boys and men.

It is clear that part of the reason for abstinence from fornication, is a means of protection from temptation and objectification. We can model chastity by wearing modest clothing, clothes that cover our cleavage and extend down to our mid-calf or knee. We can abstain from attending events that may encourage or involve crass behavior, such as hens' nights and birthday parties at clubs or pubs, especially if these events require us to go without our husbands. This is not to say we cannot go out and have fun, but simply to choose how we will have fun and with whom we will spend our time. Partaking in these kinds of events is not necessary to engage with the world. We need to be in the world but not of the world. I am by no means setting a specific standard; I am merely providing some examples and suggestions to start.

PORN IN MARRIAGE

We are among the generations that have been brought up with pornography widely accessible from any device. According to covenanteyes.com, it is believed that 64% of Christian men and 15% of Christian women watch porn once a month. It is also believed that **1 in 5 youth pastors** and **1 in 7 senior pastors** watch porn regularly. Just **55% of adults** 25 and older believe porn is wrong. We have to be aware of this. The porn habit says less about us as individuals and more about our society at large, as its usage has increased among the entire population regardless of religious or spiritual beliefs.

It's sad, but more and more, we are seeing children as young as eight being exposed to pornography. Many of us will have husbands who were exposed to porn at a young age. Any exposure can cause harm, but something especially detrimental occurs in the minds of the young. Society says it's okay, natural, and typical for boys to watch porn. We even now have girls watching it, too. Most movies and TV shows have sex scenes now. We have entered a time where exploiting another human's body is acceptable and encouraged. We've heard the phrase 'Sex sells,' which is made clear by the countless skin-thrusting advertisements forced at us daily. More and more, we see the corrupting and exploiting of our human form in order to maximize profits and sell more products. Often companies use PR to embrace political narratives currently in the limelight. They do this to enhance and justify their crude imagery, from 'my body, my choice,' to the rhetoric of 'your body is beautiful no matter what size it is.'

These advertisements pop up on our social feed and in the windows of the shops we walk past. Just as we didn't ask to see these images, most men didn't initially ask to see porn either. It was shown to them. If your husband is, or has watched it, it is essential not to be angry and aggressive with him. We must let go of the pride and hurt we feel, knowing that it is an addiction and not always an indication of our inadequacy. We must support our husbands both physically and emotionally. We must accept that we may be unable to 'fix' his issue, especially if it is some emotional coping mechanism and not merely a healthy attraction expressed poorly. Many men may find that their habit stems from a deep psychological issue that can be caused by exposure to porn or sexual acts at a young age. He may require professional help, but it is important not to push him, demand, or create ultimatums. Most men know how awful the industry is and that there are terrible things that happen to women, and they may never know if they have watched such things transpire on film; that is a fact they will have to live with. With this in mind, it's important for us to speak with our husbands in love and not disgust if this is an issue (as they may already be disgusted with themselves). Many men who do talk about this issue publicly will tell men afflicted not to talk about the issue with their partners for this very reason. I don't know about you, but I would rather know and be a support to my husband than have him keep it in the dark.

So, what can we do? We can tell our husbands that we are there for them as they need it for any purpose and especially intimacy; he only needs to ask, and even if we are tired, we can give him our word to do our best to serve his needs. If our husband is or has been afflicted by this, then he will already feel shame, especially if he is actively in the Word, and we must pray and have faith that God is with us and him and will work in time to make changes for the better. It is important to bring up this issue whether or not it causes discomfort and whether or not you are affected by it. We will not edify and correct the body of Christ if we ignore a thorn in its side, and we must be diligent and seek the truth boldly in faith if we are to actually help solve the problems we face. 1 Corinthians 7:1-8 says:

Now concerning the things whereof ye wrote unto me: It is good for a man not to touch a woman. Nevertheless, to avoid fornication, let every man have his own wife, and let every woman have her own husband. Let the husband render unto the wife due benevolence: and likewise also the wife unto the husband. The wife hath not power of her own body, but the husband: and likewise also the husband hath not power of his own body, but the wife. Defraud ye not one the other, except it be with consent for a time, that ye may give yourselves to fasting and prayer; and come together again, that Satan tempt you not for your incontinency. But I speak this by permission, and not of commandment. For I would that all men were even as I myself. But every man hath his proper gift of God, one after this manner, and another after that. I say therefore to the unmarried and widows, It is good for them if they abide even as I.

Here, Paul explains the gift that is marital sex and that it is a means of protection from temptation (1 COR 7:1-2, 5, 8-9), as well as an opportunity to give to our husbands (1 COR 7:3-5) We are our husband's just as he is ours. Our bodies are not our own. Many have taken this out of context, saying a woman should not deny her husband and that this is telling a woman that he can do whatever with her without her consent. However, this passage calls for men and women to be with one another respectfully. The husband is told to render benevolence to his wife; benevolence means kindness and charitable acts, and the same is said for the wife to her husband before any mention of the ownership of the body. This kind of care and consideration will only strengthen the marital relationship. You may have noticed that you are calmer when you have more time with your husband in an intimate setting, and the household runs smoother. If this is the case for you, imagine how that affects your family and your children's view of a marriage if you are not having those critical intimate moments with your husband.

TEACHING OUR CHILDREN TO BE CHASTE

We're encouraged to let our children have sleepovers, spend time at friends' houses without us, and go to parties and events in their most impressionable years. I am not saying we can't let our kids go to birthday parties, but I am saying that at least one parent needs to be present, and by parent, I mean you or their father. Kids get up to all sorts of mischief at parties. They find dark spots to hide in and play in, like inside closets, under tables, and areas where no one else is. In these spaces, children can easily be exposed to something they would otherwise not be: body parts, videos, images, or messages on a phone. I have spent much time telling my children that you cannot unsee something once you see it. We don't condone sleepovers, which we have explained to our children. Sleepovers are only possible if a friend's entire family unit sleeps at our home. No sleepovers are one of the most important rules we can impose as parents. I won't go into detail, but I have seen and been exposed to many things when having sleepovers with friends or spending the night at a party. Even when there was 'supervision.' I can assure you there is so much children can do in and out of eyesight without detection or repercussions. This is true in both non-religious and religious households.

Being wary or diligent about what we look at is the most important lesson to teach children today. Western culture makes being chaste a joke or a form of neglect. If a person shows modest and chaste behavior, they often get labeled as frigid, uptight, or prude. It is a source of teasing, but we cannot reduce chasteness to a joke. We want our daughters to take it seriously to avoid unwanted and unnecessary heartache or harmful memories. We can do this by educating them on marital relations and the necessity of keeping such actions between husband and wife. We can teach them the sanctity of marriage and how men and women are perfectly made to fit into one another. When your children are mature enough, you can also explain the dangers of the world and the evil one can find in men if we leave ourselves in unwed, vulnerable positions. However, just a side note: we should also warn them that marriage doesn't always save them from danger; in some cases, it is the cause, but I pray that your daughter's marriage is fruitful and her husband treats her with the meekness and adoration of a truly faithful husband...

TAKEAWAYS

- Christians should be discreet.
- Support others who are new in faith.
- Give your burdens to God.
- Be supportive of your husband, be a willing participant in intimacy.
- Speaking about your issues and annoyances to others leaves you open to bad and unbiblical advice, so be diligent and selective in your choice of council.

HEART PROBING QUESTIONS

1. How do you use social media?
2. Are you discreet in public settings? Or with family and friends?
3. Is porn in your home? If it is, how might you best support those afflicted?
4. How might you educate your children on matters of the body and being chaste?
5. Do you behave in a chaste manor?

CHAPTER 10

Keepers at Home

I want you to imagine the perfect home. What does it look like, smell like, feel like? What about the ideal you? What do you look like, act like, walk like? We can have these aspiring visions of what we want our homes or ourselves to be like, but it's important not to overindulge ourselves in ideas of perfection because perfection, though often a goal, is not attainable. I found myself in this trap. I wanted my home always to be organized, clean, and tidy, but with any number of children, wanting a home that is 'always' anything is ridiculous. Life happens at the most inconvenient times. One child might fight with another while the youngest throws up all over the couch, and the second child, the sassiest of them all, tells the two fighting to 'Stop!' in her best mummy tone, which prompts the younger of the two fighting to kick her. Such tussles can occur in the most regimented, strict, and neat homes ever to be seen because, in the end, we are but stewards and our children are free-spirited with a will of their own. If my eight years as a mother have taught me anything, it's that the seasons of life come and go, but we must be steadfast in faith, hope, and joy, determined to make our homes a beacon of light regardless of life's obstacles. Matthew 5:14-16 says:

> *Ye are the light of the world. A city that is set on an hill cannot be hid. Neither do men light a candle, and put it under a bushel, but on a candlestick; and it giveth light unto all that are in the house. Let your light so shine before men, that they may see your good works, and glorify your Father which is in heaven.*

What we do or don't do can shine a light on God and His goodness. When we diligently and mindfully care for our homes, we show care and love through our actions, creating a beautiful, calm, and loving environment for our families. I feel like this is why housekeeping is on the list of attributes and skills we younger women should possess (TIT 2:5). We can, of course, find ourselves in different housing situations, which can make the art of homemaking difficult. Believe me, I know! From a 5-bedroom house to a 2-bedroom cottage and a single room in an apartment, we have been through it all. Our constant has been our attitude and idea of what *home* means. Home for us has been wherever we are together.

DONE IS BETTER THAN PERFECT

The 'done is better than perfect' rule has been born out of the necessity to stop procrastination and settle for doing something rather than nothing. It can be overwhelming to look at the tasks before us, with the idea that we, as mothers, must do it all. However, this idea is not accurate or true. If we let go of perfection and instead delegate tasks to those who we know can do the job, even if it's not to our *standard* or liking, the job can still be done. It has been said, 'If you want a job done right, do it yourself.' To put it simply, no one will do the work exactly the way you would do it. I would flip this saying on its head and instead say, 'If you really want a job *done*, then done is better than perfect'. I've begun a new era in my home where the kids are putting up laundry, even *if* it's in a way that will take days to dry. I don't expect perfection; I just expect it to be done. In this way, I can give the children small corrections along the way. I do this in a manner that cultivates a helping attitude. When I was growing up, things had to be done in a very particular way. When something wasn't done to that exact standard, the effort was mocked. Correction is essential, but the method of correction is even more critical. We want to raise capable adults who can function in the world and not fall apart over a load of laundry, but beyond raising capable children, we want to instill in them the importance and beauty of homemaking. Showing them that the most straightforward and seemingly monotonous tasks are blessings that build strong character..

Getting Past the Feeling of Monotony

If we approach homemaking with an iterative approach, one of continual improvement, we stand to better our housekeeping methods and systems, while also understanding that the tasks we finish will be on our to-do list again and again. As soon as we tick laundry off the list, it ends up straight back at the top of the to-dos again. As much as we hate to admit it, the laundry basket will never stay empty, and the dishes will never stay done. We cannot approach homemaking as a project with a definitive end. Instead, we should view the art of housekeeping as an ongoing journey of iteration. Each time we do a task, we can get better and faster at completing it. We aren't born knowing how to fold laundry or put it out in a way that will dry. There are so many things we must learn through doing and improving.

Doing the same tasks day in and day out can lead even the most experienced homemakers to dread the day through a *rational* fear of boredom. Of course, in the home, much of what we need to do is the same one day as it was the day before. There are ways to move past this stale feeling; one is to spice things up by listening to worship music, audiobooks, or your favorite podcasts while doing your daily chores. You might also carry a notepad to write down your thoughts and epiphanies that will likely surface as you do these almost second-nature tasks. With these simple additions, those repetitive tasks can become much-needed downtime to enjoy a story, explore ideas, or practice your singing. Another way is by far the most effective in terms of mindset, and that is liturgy, making homemaking a ritual or ceremony in honor of God. Proverbs 16:3 says:

Commit thy works unto the LORD, and thy thoughts shall be established.

Of course, liturgy refers to a religious group publicly worshiping through ritual. Here, I am using the term to suggest that our homes are a way we can show our worship and devotion to God through our daily rituals in the home. We are modeling for our children, and one day, they will be guests in our homes just as we will be guests in theirs. They will reach a point where they no longer need our daily guidance and instead are leading their own children in their own way. We are establishing the rituals and rhythms of the home, and these actions we take might serve our children in their own homes with their families.

THE ACCUMULATION OF STUFF

I imagine most people nowadays have a room full of boxes of stuff they don't like or use but don't want to get rid of. Perhaps we feel bad about it and don't feel we have the time to go through it, maybe we want to keep it for a 'rainy day' or the 'what if' scenario. However, that 'what if' or 'rainy day' never comes, and we're left with a house that becomes a graveyard of discarded desires, unfinished projects, and murdered dreams, a cemetery of unfulfilled purpose. This is not the atmosphere we want in our homes, nor the environment we would want our children to be cultivated and nurtured in. Matthew 6:19-24 says:

> *Lay not up for yourselves treasures upon earth, where moth and rust doth corrupt, and where thieves break through and steal: But lay up for yourselves treasures in heaven, where neither moth nor rust doth corrupt, and where thieves do not break through nor steal: For where your treasure is, there will your heart be also. The light of the body is the*

eye: if therefore thine eye be single, thy whole body shall be full of light. But if thine eye be evil, thy whole body shall be full of darkness. If therefore the light that is in thee be darkness, how great is that darkness! No man can serve two masters: for either he will hate the one, and love the other; or else he will hold to the one, and despise the other. Ye cannot serve God and mammon.

The important thing to focus on here is precisely laying up treasures for *yourselves*. While we are imperfect beings and will always be selfish to some degree, we should exhort ourselves through faith to make appropriate decisions regarding our possessions in light of what we believe to be right, given our current revelations on the matter at hand. This will depend on the person and their circumstances. At the most basic level, a family should have a relatively safe place to eat, sleep, and raise children. We might need plates, bowls, bedsheets, and so on… In some cultures, these things may or may not be required. However, we should also remember that the things we use in our culture dictate our ability to live and provide for our family. For example, not having a fridge in a society where everyone has fridges means you can't afford to eat. You can't afford to eat without the fridge because the cultural norms that existed prior for coping with the lack of such technology, no longer exist today. So, we are therefore left individually to work out through faith and conscience what we will or won't accept in our lives, keeping in mind the well-being of our family, which is part of our duty. We already have a family to provide for, so while it may not be possible to give up as much as we might like to, what we can do is make our decisions through faith. Instead of serving and idolizing our possessions or movements such as minimalism, we use these to serve God and our family.

Living on a homestead has taught me many lessons; we've had mice, moths, ants, and maggots invade our spaces and home. We've had mice make a home in our couch and bulk-bought food items poorly stored eaten by mice, with packets left open so the food went moldy and everything else went out of date. We've had cows and pigs destroy grassed areas, welcome rugs, and the troughs we've set up for them. This constant cycle of loss on the homestead has been a deeply transformative experience; I think of these messes and the clean-up afterward whenever I want to buy something. It reminds me of the delicate nature of our doings and fleshly life; while these items may be necessary and expedient from time to time, that which we do can be undone. Now, I long for eternal treasure, the fruit of the spirit. Galatians 5:22-23 says:

> *But the fruit of the Spirit is love, joy, peace, longsuffering, gentleness, goodness, faith, Meekness, temperance: against such there is no law.*

CREATING FUNCTION

Limit screens and curate content! I wish I could shout this to the world. People say, 'you are what you eat,' but we should also say 'you become what you watch.' I want you to picture your children watching TV for the better half of the day. What do they say? What is their attitude like? I presume you have experienced something similar to me: your children look sluggish and slovenly, lolloping on the couch with their eyes fixed on the screen and vacant expressions. If you say something to them, they either don't hear you or are annoyed by your interruption. These reactions are normal for someone with screen overload. I am sure you have experienced it yourself, perhaps during a movie or series marathon on Netflix or, if you remember the DVD store days, then a marathon of what you got from the store. Your mood becomes set to that which you are watching; anxiety is often an issue. Now consider what that looks like for your home; if this is a regular occurrence, what does your home now become?

We need functioning homes. Things to do and the space to do them. Every family is different. What happens in my home might seem weird to the people in your home. Currently, we don't have a TV in our house, only computer screens, and our living room is where our office is because my husband and I spend most of our free time on creative projects. I always have a project open so I can work between everything I am doing with the children and the home throughout the day. Our children, much like us, usually sit at the table in the room next to us doing their art and craft, writing, and homeschool projects. Living this way has its own set of challenges, and I'm not suggesting you do what we do. If you've been trying to conform to the same look, style, and function of the modern home, and it hasn't been working for you, let this be the permission you need to make the changes required to suit your family's purposes. Embrace your family's different and quirky nature.

AN ALLY IN THE WAR FOR HOUSEKEEPING

Keeping house today isn't what it used to be. My kids and I have been reading The Little House In The Big Woods series and looking at the way people used to live. We have spent much time discussing the similarities and differences between now and then. Many tasks and responsibilities are the same; we still have to wash clothes, cook meals, and clean and air out the house, but how we do it is vastly different. We have vacuums and dishwashers, washing machines, and spray cleaners; we also have more affordable services to clean our homes or to bring us meals and groceries. Everything is so attainable that we don't have to spend months planning for the different seasons or treat housekeeping as an all-day career. In the times of the pioneers, technology was lacking, most work was hard work, and there was no machinery to make it easier. I can hardly imagine hunting for food before I can cook dinner or only having the option of sweeping the floor after someone tracked dirt inside, dropped food on the floor, or broke something. I don't know about you, but washing has sometimes felt like the bane of my existence. However, if I imagine what past generations had to go through for a single clean garment, it doesn't seem so bad. Can you imagine washing every item of clothing by hand? Whenever I feel annoyed by something like washing, I remind myself to be grateful for what I have and that I have a family big enough to fill my basket to overflow. If this method doesn't help you feel grateful, another way is to focus on something you enjoy first and relate it to what you're doing. For example, you could think of how much you love your child; you could imagine them laughing and smiling. Here, you can think of your children in a way that brings you joy every time you do the washing to make it a more joy-filled experience; in this way, the gratitude should come automatically with the joy, rather than trying to force a feeling of gratitude which can be a fruitless endeavor. I think we can agree, it's much harder not to be grateful for something you enjoy.

Joy and gratitude are our greatest allies in the war of housekeeping fatigue. They will safeguard our attitude and heart toward the home when society and other people discredit the art of homemaking. Most people measure success by the size of a paycheck and the house it allows them to buy. Society looks at the businesswoman with pride, while the mother at home is seen as wasted potential, lazy, and unnecessary. Proverbs 24:3-4 says:

> *Through wisdom is an house builded; and by understanding it is established: And by knowledge shall the chambers be filled with all precious and pleasant riches.*

God's word tells us that wisdom is required to build a home. We must be diligent and build our home with love and meekness. We are cultivating habits that consistently breathe life into our household and those within it. This takes patience and perseverance as we learn to unlearn the ideas of the world and embrace the beauty of the home God has given us.

God has designed us so well for our task as a helper and partner. We can build our skills and keep a home well, but we also become a home. When pregnant, our bodies become a literal home to house our growing baby. We nurture and grow life within our womb. Our body maintains and sustains life. Like our womb, our home can also sustain life. It is where our family assembles, prays, plays, and grows together. Just as the home can be life-sustaining, it can also be draining. We, along with our husbands, build the foundations of our home. We must take care of any cracks in the foundation so they don't become big cracks. It may be tempting to look around at other mothers who seem to have it all figured out with a neat, tidy, and regimented home, but the truth is we all have messes to clean up. The house can never be clean every moment of every day, and the only secret to a tidy and organized home is action. The power is in action. If we are idle, our house will fall, but when we are diligent, we build our home and cultivate a lasting legacy.

We can all admit that we have scrolled through Instagram at some point and seen an image of a mother or a home that we are envious of; we weren't thinking, 'Well done, you,' or 'How blessed your family is.' No. We were thinking of ourselves, how our home doesn't look that way, and how we wish it would. But wishing and wanting don't make something happen. Action does. That action needs to come from a place of good intent; otherwise, it can quickly become a spiraling force of darkness that sweeps through your home. Perfectionism takes over next to envy, and soon, you will be serving two masters. Because our treasure is that of our character, we must focus on and cultivate that through faith and the Word, so we don't fall into the trap of leaning on our understanding. Proverbs 3:3-8 says:

Let not mercy and truth forsake thee: bind them about thy neck; write them upon the table of thine heart: So shalt thou find favour and good understanding in the sight of God and man. Trust in the LORD with all thine heart; and lean not unto thine own understanding. In all thy ways acknowledge him, and he shall direct thy path. Be not wise in thine own eyes: fear the LORD, and depart from evil. It shall be health to thy navel, and marrow to thy bones.

Scripture can be like a shield if we take the time to read and memorize it. Here are some verses that come to my mind when I feel I am being tested: Philippians 4:8, 1 Corinthians 6:19-20 and 10:31, Proverbs 3:5, and Ephesians 2:8-9. Regarding the home, we understand that it is one of many God-given duties. Homemaking is our jurisdiction and a task in much need of a woman's touch. We beautify and glorify God through our home and our nature. I've noted on many occasions how calm the children are when the house is tidy and how content my husband is when the floor is clear and the surfaces are clean. There is something to be said about the peace a clean and tidy home can bring.

If we look to an untidy home and its impacts, we see more messes created, more arguments, and less restful sleep and sabbaths. A home can get out of control with all the items that accumulate inside it, taking up valuable space and time. Managing a home is part of shepherding our children. It shows them how to care for and look after what we are given by God.

USING OUR BLESSINGS

The parable of 'A Nobleman's Ten Pounds' Luke chapter 19:11-26 says:

> *And as they heard these things, he added and spake a parable, because he was nigh to Jerusalem, and because they thought that the kingdom of God should immediately appear. He said therefore, A certain nobleman went into a far country to receive for himself a kingdom, and to return. And he called his ten servants, and delivered them ten pounds, and said unto them, Occupy till I come. But his citizens hated him, and sent a message after him, saying, We will not have this man to reign over us. And it came to pass, that when he was returned, having received the kingdom, then he commanded these servants to be called unto him, to whom he had given the money, that he might know how much every man had*

gained by trading. Then came the first, saying, Lord, thy pound hath gained ten pounds. And he said unto him, Well, thou good servant: because thou hast been faithful in a very little, have thou authority over ten cities. And the second came, saying, Lord, thy pound hath gained five pounds. And he said likewise to him, Be thou also over five cities. And another came, saying, Lord, behold, here is thy pound, which I have kept laid up in a napkin: For I feared thee, because thou art an austere man: thou takest up that thou layedst not down, and reapest that thou didst not sow. And he saith unto him, Out of thine own mouth will I judge thee, thou wicked servant. Thou knewest that I was an austere man, taking up that I laid not down, and reaping that I did not sow: Wherefore then gavest not thou my money into the bank, that at my coming I might have required mine own with usury? And he said unto them that stood by, Take from him the pound, and give it to him that hath ten pounds. (And they said unto him, Lord, he hath ten pounds.) For I say unto you, That unto every one which hath shall be given; and from him that hath not, even that he hath shall be taken away from him.

We are given gifts from God and opportunities to use those gifts; here, it is made clear that we should use our talents consciously and diligently. We cannot hide away. We all have different gifts, and perhaps some are more profitable than others, but we are to do whatever task is set before us with the attention and care we would give to anything the LORD had directly asked us to do. Small and simple tasks can be done lovingly for the LORD, unlike the man given the least in the parable, who, judging over the Lord's character, acted out of fear for his own sake. This includes washing the dishes, loading the washing machine, and other seemingly small household tasks. It is also essential to note that every little task has a significant impact. If you don't wash your dishes, the dishes will pile up, cover the counters, and make it impossible to prepare a meal; the dishes will also be more challenging to clean as the food sets to stone. The little tasks done consistently make way for big rewards. Our homes must be working homes, active with routines and systems. And remember, these routines and systems are there to serve us and God! Not us serve them. I cannot stress this point enough, lest the routine becomes your focus rather than God and family!

We should treat each kind of gift or talent as God-given; using it rightly to glorify and increase our family's profitability. It's clear that we are meant to run the home, but you may also feel called to do something else. In this, we can pray, dabble, and explore those desires to write a book, start a mother's group, do business, or help the local community. Whatever it is, the only way to know if it's right for you and your family is if you begin the work. We can look to Proverbs 31 for inspiration in homemaking and utilization of God-given talents. Proverbs 31:10-31 tells us the value of such a godly woman:

> *Who can find a virtuous woman? for her price is far above rubies. The heart of her husband doth safely trust in her, so that he shall have no need of spoil. She will do him good and not evil all the days of her life. She seeketh wool, and flax, and worketh willingly with her hands. She is like the merchants' ships; she bringeth her food from afar. She riseth also while it is yet night, and giveth meat to her household, and a portion to her maidens. She considereth a field, and buyeth it: with the fruit of her hands she planteth a vineyard. She girdeth her loins with strength, and strengtheneth her arms. She perceiveth that her merchandise is good: her candle goeth not out by night. She layeth her hands to the spindle, and her hands hold the distaff. She stretcheth out her hand to the poor; yea, she reacheth forth her hands to the needy. She is not afraid of the snow for her household: for all her household are clothed with scarlet. She maketh herself coverings of tapestry; her clothing is silk and purple. Her husband is known in the gates, when he*

sitteth among the elders of the land. She maketh fine linen, and selleth it; and delivereth girdles unto the merchant. Strength and honour are her clothing; and she shall rejoice in time to come. She openeth her mouth with wisdom; and in her tongue is the law of kindness. She looketh well to the ways of her household, and eateth not the bread of idleness. Her children arise up, and call her blessed; her husband also, and he praiseth her. Many daughters have done virtuously, but thou excellest them all. Favour is deceitful, and beauty is vain: but a woman that feareth the LORD, she shall be praised. Give her of the fruit of her hands; and let her own works praise her in the gates.

These verses speak of a virtuous woman and her value to her family. We know the Proverbs 31 woman doesn't exist, but the example given works as a perfect ideal. We can know this because 31:12 says: 'She will do him good and not evil all the days of her life.' This is impossible as we are both flesh and spirit. Evil is sin, and sin can be in thought or deed. There is no way that any wife will not sin against her husband in either thought or deed all the days of her life; even the slightest hint of anger for a nano-second towards the husband would not be possible for the Proverbs 31 woman. I say all this to make sure we keep a humble spirit before I move on, acknowledging the truth while also striving for greatness in love. Proverbs 31 shows us the potential of what a woman could be; she takes care of her home and is then driven and fruitful in business. She brings honor and makes her house profitable. This woman is diligent and prepared for the different seasons and possible problems ahead. She rises early and goes to bed late. It's important to note here that not all of us are designed to write a book, take on some wild business venture, or grow a vineyard, but there is something that every one of us uniquely brings to this world. Your life's journey thus far has made you who you are, and wherever you go depends on the choices you make here now and onward. If you feel your place is in the home serving your family only, then own it, work it, and know that what you do is fantastic; if you feel that you're meant to juggle and take on entrepreneurship, do that, be courageous, and make those decisions. The Proverbs 31 woman shows what could be possible for us in our life as mothers. We can meditate on this and use her as an example to lead us beyond our reserved judgments about what we think is possible for us to accomplish.

ACTIONABLE CHANGE

Knowing what to say yes and no to is a skill you can learn to master when you begin to write down what you feel called to do. You can discover why it is essential and how you might achieve your life goals before breaking them down into small, accomplishable actions. Little and often. This is a must-remember motto. Everything you do to improve your circumstances and your home functionality will compound to make significant differences. There are seasons when we can do more and have a massive cleanup and organization of our life or home in a short time span. Then there are seasons where little is possible that's not related to keeping everyone fed and watered; here we can make profoundly significant impacts through the small actions we take daily and pave the way for substantial actions in the future.

These little actions are habits. Habits are things that many gurus, teachers, and philosophers talk about. Our habits form from our upbringing, society, or purely by necessity; as Christians, we must take control of our habits to guide and form them intentionally. For instance, one could create a habit where a meal is made on the Sabbath, and the Bible is read. Perhaps this gathering will be your family unit, or you will bring together extended family or the community. We can build traditions and lasting habits that our children will cherish through small actions toward bigger goals. We must look at habits as things we must form through iterations; constant growth and change are required, and we must also be careful about adhering to traditions for the serving of the tradition itself; it should serve us in our journey to grow in love and faith toward God…

TAKE AWAYS

- Reduce the amount of stuff in your home.
- Turn off the TV and tune out of social media to reduce the amount of stuff coming into your home if you find there is too much.
- Let go of perfection, embrace action.
- Slowly build good habits within the home

HEART PROBING QUESTIONS

1. Is your home manageable? Or cluttered?
2. Are you expecting or envisioning perfection for your home?
3. Do you overconsume?
4. How might you reduce your consumption of needless goods?

CHAPTER 11

The Word of God Be Not Blasphemed

Actions speak louder than words, a picture is worth a thousand words, and home is where the heart is. We are representatives of God on Earth. When we claim to be Christian or to believe in the Lord, our character represents Christ to the unbeliever whether we want it to or not, whether we reflect Him or not. Titus 2:5 says, "*To be* discreet, chaste, keepers at home, good, obedient to their own husbands, that the word of God be not blasphemed." In this verse, Paul refers to the exhortations he has laid out. A failure in these teachings would reflect onto Christ, the Church, and Christianity as a whole (Matthew 5:16.) It is easy to see the mundane chores, modest dress, etc., as unimportant, but those small tasks are of great importance. Luke 16:10 says:

> *He that is faithful in that which is least is faithful also in much: and he that is unjust in the least is unjust also in much.*

The home can often be seen as the least important thing we do due to the many little tasks that make the running of a home smooth, but every little job and action adds up to something grander and more significant. It's essential to know that your impact on the world can be profound through doing the mundane exceedingly well, for these things faithfully done change the lives of those in your household, and they will one day be out in the world. They, too, will cause an effect, and we want that effect to be for His glory. Romans 2:24 says:

> *For the name of God is blasphemed among the Gentiles through you, as it is written.*

It is our actions, words, and lifestyle that represent Christ. We represent Him because we proclaim His name. We profess our love and followership. This then shows others what following Christ looks like and the results of following Him. That's not to say anyone should expect to prosper and have worldly goods if they love God. However, we should aim to grow in and show the fruit of the Spirit. Those fruits should help us walk in the Spirit while faithfully stewarding our homes, marriage, and children. The changes that occur within us through our love of Christ and the Holy Spirit are what we want to speak the loudest. It is the noisiest part of us that will catch people's attention, so if the mess of your home is obscene, it may speak the loudest. We don't have to be perfect. Perfection isn't possible anyway. But we must act in faith and know we represent Him when we proclaim His name.

Our children are in our charge. We are to teach them. They're watching whether we are faithful in the small things. We have been given the extraordinary task and blessing of raising children. This is such a sacred blessing that God has entrusted us with. Let us embrace this.

GETTING PAST PRIDE

'Why God? Why?' We've all had moments of looking up at the sky and asking this, usually when things seem hard to handle or unfair. The 'why me' can often be a prideful call to God saying 'I don't deserve this.' But of course, we are all sinners. We all do wrong, and we don't always have an idea or understanding of the true repercussions. And so here I must stress that we ought to humble ourselves even when we are angry with God or our situation, remembering that none are good and all of us fall short of the glory of God. This also doesn't mean you are directly responsible for a calamity in your life and here we can look to the book of Job as an example. We need to remain humble and faithful and know that God works all things for good as he is good and any evil that is allowed now will ultimately be made up for in the future.

We can and should come to God with whatever we think or feel; we can let go of resentment, fear, and anger even if we feel these things toward Him. When we let go, we uncover the genuine desire and need for comfort, love, and to be known. In these humbling moments, we can truly grow and connect with God. We don't have to hide the bad days or our anger from Him. He still loves us, and although we may think about it and say it sometimes, He won't forsake us. Even Jesus asked why God had forsaken him. Matthew 27:45-46 says:

> *Now from the sixth hour there was darkness over all the land unto the ninth hour. And about the ninth hour Jesus cried with a loud voice, saying, **Eli, Eli, lama sabachthani?** that is to say, My God, my God, why hast thou forsaken me?*

As Christians, we want to be like Christ, and one of the best ways to do that is by having conversations with God even in our darkest moments.

ATTRIBUTION AND DECLARATION

As mentioned, coming to God and talking to Him, whether in prayer or thought, is an important part of our Christian journey. However, we need to address the significant number of women in the world claiming to know God's thoughts and desires *for them*. I have noticed these declarations prominently in women of faith who run faith-based businesses, social media accounts, etc. Someone even went as far as to say that her business is God's, that she has handed it to God. I understand the sentiment and the wish to hand over control to God, but we can't force God to take our responsibilities. What we do and say matters; we don't want to say something is from Him if it isn't. We can get lost in fantasy, caught up in signs, of dreams and thoughts, but Isaiah 55:6-12 says:

> *Seek ye the LORD while he may be found, call ye upon him while he is near: Let the wicked forsake his way, and the unrighteous man his thoughts: and let him return unto the LORD, and he will have mercy upon him; and to our God, for he will abundantly pardon. For my thoughts **are** not your*

thoughts, neither are your ways my ways, saith the LORD. For as the heavens are higher than the earth, so are my ways higher than your ways, and my thoughts than your thoughts. For as the rain cometh down, and the snow from heaven, and returneth not thither, but watereth the earth, and maketh it bring forth and bud, that it may give seed to the sower, and bread to the eater: So shall my word be that goeth forth out of my mouth: it shall not return unto me void, but it shall accomplish that which I please, and it shall prosper in the thing whereto I sent it. For ye shall go out with joy, and be led forth with peace: the mountains and the hills shall break forth before you into singing, and all the trees of the field shall clap their hands.

Our thoughts are not His, and our dreams are also not His; we must be careful not to attribute and declare our understandings or ever-changing emotions with His path for us (Proverbs 3:5-6). If God wants you to do something, He will make it abundantly clear to you just as He did to Moses through the burning bush, Mary when the Angels visited her, David when he heard Goliath and was convicted to fight him, and Jonah when he faced a terrible storm and was swallowed up by the fish. You will not have to fear whether you are hearing God if He speaks to you; have faith and know that He will guide your path. God is not the one to confuse 1 Corinthians 14:33 says:

> *For God is not **the author** of confusion, but of peace, as in all churches of the saints.*

FOLLOWER OF CHRIST

Remember when you were a child and every new acquaintance was your best friend? You had known this new person for only five minutes, but it felt like years, and soon, you were sharing a sandwich and a chocolate bar. Children are so open and willing to love when young. We should embrace this kind of love and willingness to share and be open with God. Ongoing conversation and prayer with God will enable us to get to know Him and feel closer to Him. Seek and ye shall find (MAT 7:7). Cultivating a relationship with God should help us walk in the spirit, make better decisions, and embody the character of a godly woman. We want to be able to say to our children confidently 1 Corinthians 11:1 says:

> *Be ye followers of me, even as I also am of Christ.*

Paul was a follower of Christ, and we, too, must be if we are to lead our children correctly. All that we have discussed in Titus 2 leads us to this Christ-like motherhood that shines a light in the darkness and leads the way to our loving God. 1 John 4: 7-11 says:

Beloved, let us love one another: for love is of God; and every one that loveth is born of God, and knoweth God. He that loveth not knoweth not God; for God is love. In this was manifested the love of God toward us, because that God sent his only begotten Son into the world, that we might live through him. Herein is love, not that we loved God, but that he loved us, and sent his Son to be the propitiation for our sins. Beloved, if God so loved us, we ought also to love one another.

We are the nurturers, the cultivators of life and life-giving fruit. We are our husbands' helpers, his confidant, his best friend. We are willing to sacrifice for the LORD on Earth so His works might be performed through us. We can be a godly anchor and light, standing steadfast in faith. Be brave, be courageous, and be encouraged by the position God has chosen for you, for only you can fulfill His requirements in the way you would do it…

TAKEAWAYS

- Motherhood is a sacred duty and should be treasured and carried out like any work for the LORD
- Your thoughts are your own.
- Do not proclaim to know Gods thoughts or plans for you or that He is in charge of your work.

HEART PROBING QUESTIONS

1. How do you feel about motherhood?
2. Have you ever attributed something to God that you shouldn't?

CHAPTER 12

The Seasons of Motherhood

Looking around the home, we mothers might get discouraged with the dishes piling up and a laundry basket that never gets empty. Every meal that is made and finished leads into the next meal as you cook and clean between feeding and nap times. We mother in seasons. Sometimes, your current season might be busier than the last. Babies require more physical constant care than teens. Teens need more conversation and teachings into adulthood (or at least the environment to learn from their mistakes as safely as possible). Often, we want to bubble wrap our children to protect them from every danger; of course, one day, they will need to be in the world and be able to live in the world as lights. Today, we have youth that are unable to cope with life because they have been raised by misguided, sometimes well-meaning, teachers and coddled by their parents. We are in this time through the actions and choices of the many. I pray that you may be one of the growing few who take it upon themselves to become this Titus 2 Mother focused on pleasing Him and doing all for Him, having faith in His goodness and His faithfulness. Let us be the nurturing army of God that helps lead our children to Him and prepares them for the world. (MAT 5:14-16)

A non-Christian friend asked me about this book and the difference between Christian motherhood and 'motherhood.' To this, I answered contentment and comfort. When you have faith, you have a love you *know* exists. I told her that even though she did not believe, God still loves her now and always, no matter what she has done or does. This is the comfort we Christians have; we know that no matter what we do or don't do, God loves us, Christ died for us, and He has by grace given us through faith the free gift of everlasting life.

NUMBER YOUR DAYS

We must never forget that busy days will one day be memories, ones we will look back on. One day, our children will be old, and we will be older, looking upon them and their children. They will be guests in our home, and we will be guests in theirs. I took some time to count my days, to look at my family's ages for the next twenty years, seeing what age we will all be and when, and my goodness! It put life into perspective. Psalm 90:12 says:

So teach us to number our days, that we may apply our hearts unto wisdom

When you put your time into numbers, the clarity of how little time we truly have becomes clearer. So many people spend their lives trying to accumulate things, seeking happiness, and acquiring riches, but the true richness of life lies in the growth of the spirit and the lives we touch.

With every word and teaching in this book, it's essential to understand that I'm not writing from a place of wealth and abundance. I live on an off-grid farm in the Australian Wheatbelt. We experience severe heat and drought, along with summer storms and flood-causing rains in the winter. We don't own this place; we are here as caretakers. As such, we have learned and grown a great deal. Because we are so far out in the sticks, or the wilderness as I call it, we are quite isolated from family and friends. It has been both a curse and a blessing, but I know God has placed us here for a reason, and His plans are better than ours.

Here is where I came, naive to the pain of actual loss, and here is where that naivety was shattered as I lost two precious and beloved babies. But here is also where my heart healed, and I experienced my redeeming childbirth; here is where Grace was born, and my living children crowded around her and me to get a peek at the newest member of our family. Here is where we fit our family of six, seven including Alfie, into a two-bedroom cottage. We live on top of each other, but somehow, even in times of overwhelm, we get through.

It is the little things that make growing up special. It's the crowding around and holding one another. The goodnight kisses, the bedtime stories, and the late nights watching thunderstorms out of the floor-to-ceiling glass doors on a weeknight because school is at home the next day and there is no hard and fast start time. It is running outside to see the piglets that have just been born, the moody mama pig who almost squishes her babies by sitting on them, and the life lesson that nature isn't kind or fair. Still, it is what it is, and terrible things can happen, like the two piglets that didn't survive after birth or the two who did get flattened by their mother's weight on top of them. There is horror amidst the beauty.

We feel love in memorable moments when conversations flow, arms are outstretched, and we are there to look and listen. We feel love when we think of the Father, the Son, and the Spirit, or those who have gone before us and are awaiting us in heaven. Love fills us when we pray, and gratitude helps us stay humble in a world where pride is quickly celebrated. We are called to become Titus 2 Mothers so we can lay the foundations for cultivating a family culture that transcends, nurtures, and guides God's people to Him.

TAKEAWAYS

- Motherhood is a blessing from the LORD may we treasure it and live out His teachings, shining a light to Him so that the lost may be found.
- May we grow in motherhood little by little cultivating lasting change and habits to Glorify Him.
- Let us number our days with strength and diligence that our time here is short but also with great joy knowing eternity is forever.

HEART PROBING QUESTIONS

1. How will you use the teachings in this book to help you in your life?
2. How has this book affected you and your outlook?
3. What is the biggest takeaway you have found in this book?

Bibliography

Margaret Sanger and H. G. Wells "The Pivot of Civilization" Released Feb 22, 2006

Margaret Sanger "A Plan for Peace" Birth Control Review April 1932, pp. 107-108

Edward L. Bernays "Propaganda" 1928

TIME "Sugar can be the Willpower You Need to Undereat" ad May 10, 1971

L&M filter tip cigarettes "Just What the Doctor Ordered" ad

Dean Ornish "Love and Survival: The Scientific Basis for the Healing Power of Intimacy" 1998

ELLA ROSE

Ella Rose Roussel mama of 4 wife to her high school
sweetheart, hosts two podcasts and a blog where she
speaks with men and women around the world about
parenting, pregnancy loss and much more. She also has a
community coming soon for all mamas to join and feel
connected to like minded women who will support each other
in faith, life and motherhood.

www.HeyBeautifulMama.com
@HeyBeautifulMama

TRUTH
BE TOLD

At Truth Be Told Publishing we're on a mission to bring you wholesome books that will edify, guide, bring joy and inspire young and old minds. Join our mission by visiting our website below and be the first to know about new releases.

www.TruthBeToldPublishing.com

Printed in the USA
CPSIA information can be obtained
at www.ICGtesting.com
CBHW020510150624
10005CB00004B/116